ALA READERS' ADVISORY SERIES

Serving Boys through Readers' Advisory

The Readers' Advisory Guide to Graphic Novels

The Readers' Advisory Guide to Genre Fiction,
second edition

Research-Based Readers' Advisory

The Readers' Advisory Guide to Nonfiction

Serving Teens through Readers' Advisory

The Horror Readers' Advisory:
The Librarian's Guide to Vampires, Killer Tomatoes,
and Haunted Houses

The Science Fiction and Fantasy Readers' Advisory:
The Librarian's Guide to Cyborgs, Aliens,
and Sorcerers

The Mystery Readers' Advisory:
The Librarian's Clues to Murder and Mayhem

The Romance Readers' Advisory:
The Librarian's Guide to Love in the Stacks

The Short Story Readers' Advisory: A Guide to the Best

The Readers' Advisory Handbook

EDITED BY

Jessica E. Moyer

and

Kaite Mediatore Stover

American Library Association

Chicago   2010

Jessica E. Moyer has MS and CAS degrees from the University of Illinois, Graduate School of Library and Information Science. She has published articles in *Reference and User Services Quarterly, New Library World,* and the *Libraries Unlimited Readers' Advisor Newsletter;* she is the author of *Research-Based Readers' Advisory* (2008); and she is the editor of the *Journal of Research on Libraries and Young Adults.* An active member of ALA, Moyer is currently a member of the editorial boards for *Reference and User Services Quarterly* and *Booklist's Reference Books Bulletin* and is chair of the 2010 RUSA Awards committee. She reviews fiction, audiobooks, reference books, and professional reading for *Booklist* and fiction for *Library Journal.* In 2008 she was named a *Library Journal* Mover and Shaker.

Kaite Mediatore Stover is the head of readers' services for the Kansas City (Missouri) Public Library. She holds a master's degree in library science and a master's degree in literature from Emporia (Kansas) State University. Stover is the "She Reads" columnist and an audiobook reviewer for *Booklist* and a contributing writer for NoveList, and she has contributed articles to *Reference and User Services Quarterly.* She is active in ALA and has served on the *Booklist* Advisory Board, the PLA Readers' Advisory Committee, the RUSA CODES Readers' Advisory Committee, YALSA's Alex Awards Committee, and the Sophie Brody Medal Committee. In 2003 she was named one of *Library Journal's* Movers and Shakers.

The paper used in this publication meets the minimum requirements of American National Standard for Information Sciences—Permanence of Paper for Printed Library Materials, ANSI Z39.48-1992. ∞

Library of Congress Cataloging-in-Publication Data
The readers' advisory handbook / edited by Jessica E. Moyer and Kaite Mediatore Stover.
    p.   cm. — (ALA readers' advisory series)
Includes bibliographical references and index.
ISBN 978-0-8389-1042-9 (alk. paper)
    1. Readers' advisory services—United States. I. Moyer, Jessica E. II. Stover, Kaite Mediatore.
    Z711.55.R44 2010
    025.5'4—dc22   2009045793

ISBN-13: 978-0-8389-1042-9

Printed in the United States of America

14   13   12   11   10   5   4   3   2   1

CONTENTS

ACKNOWLEDGMENTS

First and foremost, heartfelt thanks to my coeditor, Kaite Stover. Without her hard work in finding authors and reading and rereading the chapters, this project would not have turned out nearly so well. I think we're both glad I twisted her arm to be my coeditor and take on such a big project. I know I'm really glad we were able to work together.

J. Michael Jeffers at ALA Editions not only has been a great editor but has been supportive of this idea from the very beginning and gave much-needed encouragement to get this book done on time. Thanks to Michael and all the other staff at ALA Editions who've helped out, from editing to marketing.

I also owe a great deal to the many authors who shared their expertise and time to contribute chapters on a wide range of readers' advisory topics. Their frontline experience and day-to-day experiences working with readers are what really make this book a valuable resource for librarians.

Last, I must thank my family for giving me the time and space to work on this project for the last two years. My husband not only listened to me talk and talk and talk about this but also cooked dinner and was understanding when I dedicated entire weekends to book work, not housework. My cats, Mitt, Tiggy, and Smokey, kept me company while I worked and provided much-needed hugs and love, and my dog, Callie, made me take walk breaks.

—Jessica

I don't think I can thank Jessica Moyer enough for persuading me to work on this project with her. It's easy to look back now through rose-tinted specs and say it was a cakewalk from the very beginning. But even the hard work was less formidable when the two of us tackled it together.

The other Jessica in my life, Jessica Zellers, deserves much appreciation for taking time from her own editing to swap baldly honest e-mails about the writing process. The workloads were always a little lighter after these caffeine-enabled Sunday afternoon exchanges.

I can't express enough gratitude to the contributors who all said yes without reservation and turned in sensational work. Special nods to Erin, Alicia, Kate, and CJ for stepping in at the last minute.

My family and friends can never be repaid for all the times they dropped their guard and asked me, "Whatcha been doing?" and then listened to the details of the book's progress (without letting their eyes glaze over) and my hollow promises to "come up for air at the end of this month, I swear."

I am grateful to the Kansas City Public Library for creating an environment that supports, encourages, and appreciates professional development. Lillie Brack gave me all the time off I needed (usually at the last minute) to write. Many thanks to the customer service staff at KCPL: Ann, Bill, Tom, Kelly, Stephanie, Kathleen, Topher, and Lindsee. I owe big plates of gratitude to Bill Ott at *Booklist* and Katherine Johnson at NoveList, who let me slide on all kinds of writing assignments to get this big one out of the way.

While he thinks he didn't have "a damn thing to do with it," my husband, Mike Stover, is correct in a sense. There's nothing of him in this book. Just like there's nothing of me in any of his musical compositions. But someone had to do the cooking, keep the cats fed, and buy me a new laptop. Most important, whenever I gave in to the little demons and despaired whether this thing would ever be done and who the hell did I think I was anyway to do a book, what am I crazy or something, I can't do this, he'd look at me calmly and say, "Yes, you can."

Of course, my half of this book is for Mike, Mom, and Dad. Without whom, nothing.

—Kaite

INTRODUCTION

It almost seems ludicrous to point out that libraries have seen a tremendous growth in services to readers. What *else* would a library be doing if not serving readers? Yet as many dedicated staff and loyal patrons know, this ain't your grandma's "liberry" anymore. Between the homework help centers, computer classes, job search training, and a plethora of other programs and services too numerous to count, libraries are seeing a significant increase in the use of all services, especially in this unpredictable economic climate. In addition to the uptick in everyday library traffic, staff are seeing workloads broadening, services expanding, and budgets tightening. This translates to less time and fewer resources for training, continuing education, and professional development off-site.

One of the fastest-growing services in libraries is readers' advisory. This service has long since sprinted past merely suggesting books to faithful library patrons while chatting at the circulation desk. Readers' advisory encompasses many different leisure reading formats and means of communication, and working with patrons of all types and ages, in and outside the library. Books will always hold pride of place among readers' advisors and library patrons. But the volcanic increase in digital formats, higher demand for programming, and savvier promotional materials require new skills and tools for library staff dedicated to serving their readers in the best ways possible. *The Readers' Advisory Handbook* is an introductory resource designed to be used by anyone involved in readers' advisory, but one that we hope will be especially helpful to students in readers' advisory courses, new librarians, and all library staff involved in readers' advisory services. With a practice-oriented focus, the *RA Handbook* will help staff and librarians answer day-to-day RA service dilemmas and questions, such as How do I create a good display? How do I make a read-alike list? How do I write an audiobook review? These are basic skills every member of a library's RA team should possess.

Almost all the skills, techniques, and practices presented in this book have been included in a briefer form in workshops or seminars or both on basic readers' advisory training. But we know that only a minority of library staff providing readers' advisory services are actually able to attend these events. Even those lucky enough to attend might only be able to work with their new knowledge if they take detailed notes. This book is intended to be a one-stop source for all kinds of basic readers' advisory issues, from learning how to read a book in ten minutes to creating read-alike lists. Besides covering the basics, there are chapters on more elaborate library programming that serves the reading interests of patrons. Author visits and book groups, both mainstays of library programming, receive detailed treatments that will not only instruct a newcomer but offer refresher training for programming veterans. Storytelling has never fallen out of fashion for children and is now moving on to a more adult audience. See how to craft an inexpensive, high-impact program that will amuse adults and draw them back into the world of story. Readers' advisory services are also expanding to assist more specialized audiences. This book includes expert guidance on providing services to senior citizens, teens, and readers who are incarcerated.

The book is organized into five parts. Part 1, "Getting to Know Your Materials," is about becoming better acquainted with the collections that are the foundation for readers' advisory, including fiction, nonfiction, audiobooks, and graphic novels. The last chapter in this section covers genre studies as a way for readers' advisors to study their collections in depth. Part 2, "Reviewing and Evaluating Materials," includes chapters on writing reviews and annotations for fiction and nonfiction, audiobooks, graphic novels, and reference materials. Part 3, "Marketing, Promoting, and Sharing Materials," gets into the important day-to-day work of advisors: creating booklists, bookmarks, displays, themed booklists, read-alikes, and book group kits. The last chapter in this section addresses the critical area of websites and readers' advisory in an electronic world. Part 4, "Programming," opens with a primer on book groups, moves to the increasingly popular author event, and closes with a chapter on storytelling programs for adults. The final part, "Expanding Readers' Services," covers unique situations, including readers' advisory by proxy, readers' advisory for older adults, readers' advisory for incarcerated populations, and crossover readers' advisory (suggesting young adult books to adult readers and working with teens who enjoy reading adult books).

Each chapter breaks down the step-by-step methods for a variety of readers' advisory skills and services. Worksheets are included in many chapters to help you develop and practice the skill or service. These chapters can be used as single courses of study for the eager readers' advisor or adapted for in-library staff development training or department meetings. Chapters are designed to be read alone or as part of their larger section.

Feel free to skip straight to the chapter(s) that best address your needs, or, if you are new to RA, reading the book straight through will provide an excellent introduction to the field.

Both new and seasoned library staff in public or school libraries will find ways to create, revitalize, or expand services to readers with *The Readers' Advisory Handbook*. Once these missions have been accomplished, we encourage you to share all your experiences, tips, successes, and failures with other library staff. We are all only as good as the shared body of knowledge.

Part 1

Getting to Know Your Materials

1

HOW TO READ A BOOK IN TEN MINUTES

Jessica E. Moyer

One of the easiest ways to get to know your collections is to use the "Read a Book in Ten Minutes" strategy. This standard RA technique has been taught in numerous workshops and conference programs and is considered a basic element of a readers' advisor's skill set. The late Jane Hirsch of the Montgomery County (Maryland) Department of Public Libraries was one of the original developers of these guidelines, which were later expanded by Lisa Sampley (Springfield-Greene County [Missouri] Library) and published in *Missouri Library World*.[1] Mary K. Chelton and Joyce Saricks made further modifications for their workshops and presentations. The guidelines draw on all these forebears as well as on Saricks's descriptions of appeal factors from the 2005 edition of *Readers' Advisory Service in the Public Library*.[2]

To get started, grab a book you haven't read before, by an author you don't know, and preferably one that you don't intend to read later. Advance reading copies or editions (ARC or ARE) are good options as long as they include full-color covers, descriptions, and author information. As you follow the steps listed here, be sure to make notes. Remember, you have only ten minutes, so read and write quickly! Use the worksheet at the end of the chapter as a guide and a place to take notes.

HOW TO READ A BOOK IN TEN MINUTES: EIGHT EASY STEPS

1. Start with the cover: all the colors, images, and text on the cover are meant to convey a message. These elements are critical in the publisher's marketing of the book and can tell a reader a lot. What does the cover tell you about the book?

    a. Do the cover images look like they are aimed at a particular sex or age?

    b. Is the cover image off-putting to its intended audience or obviously dated?

    c. Does it give you an idea of the potential readership or genre?

    d. What does the cover say about the author? Has he or she won any awards?

    e. Is the author's name or title in larger print? A very large name is a good clue that this author might be a best seller.

    f. Is an unusual font or color used? Bright red text that drips like blood would be a good indication that this is a scary book.

2. Open the book and read the jacket blurb or the back cover or both.

    a. What does the blurb or cover tell you about the book? Is a plot summary given? Is the book directly compared to any other books?

    b. What about the author? Is a bio given or a list of previous books?

    c. What do other authors think of this book? Who are those authors? Use these to help you start making read-alike connections.

3. Flip to a random page. Check the typeface.

    a. How easy is it to read?

    b. Is the typeface better for younger or older readers?

    c. Is there anything especially noticeable or unusual?

    d. Is more than one typeface used?

    e. Are there illustrations? Do they have captions or enhance the text? Do they add to the overall story? Are they an integral part of the story?

4. Check the physical characteristics.

    a. Heft: Can readers easily carry the book? How big and heavy is it?

    b. Will the intended audience be willing or able to hold the book and carry it around?

    c. Is it hardcover or paperback or mass market?

    d. Can the book be easily opened while reading?

5. Read a sample.

    a. Read the first chapter. What happens at the very beginning? Which characters or what setting is introduced? How does the story start—with a description or with action?

    b. Read some pages in the middle. Are the same characters or setting still present? What kinds of events are taking place? Is the text mostly dialogue or mostly description? How much white space is on the page?

c. Read the last chapter (this is why it is best to choose a book you don't actually plan on reading). How does the story end? Is the ending resolved? Left wide open? Left a little open with room for a sequel? Is it a cliffhanger that demands a sequel? Who is still alive/giving the final speech?

6. Consider the book's appeal factors.

a. Pacing: How quickly are characters and plot revealed? Is there more dialogue or more description? Check for white space; the more dialogue, the more white space. Are there short sentences, short paragraphs, and short chapters? The shorter the sentences, chapters, and paragraphs, the faster it will read. Are there multiple plotlines, flashbacks, or different points of view, or does the book have a linear plot? Is the ending open or closed?

b. Frame: Is the background detailed or minimal? How is the book supposed to make the reader feel? Is a special background integral to understanding the story? Is the reader assumed to have certain types of knowledge—for example, subject information essential to full understanding or previous knowledge of the world in which the story takes place (e.g., books in a series)?

c. Story line: Does the story emphasize people or events? Is the focus interior/psychological or exterior/action? What is the author's intent—serious versus light; comedy versus drama?

d. Characterization: Are characters fully developed or are they easily recognized types? Is the focus on a single character or on several who intertwine? Is characterization the most important aspect of the story? Are characters developed during the series or in one book? Are there memorable or important secondary characters?

e. What's the most important or most dominant appeal factor?

7. Consider other factors.

a. Plot: What is the book actually about? Can you summarize the book in thirty seconds or less? If someone asked you, "What is this book about," how would you respond?

b. Genre: Is the book part of a recognized genre? If so, which one? What about subgenre? Is it a genre blend? Does the book conform to genre formulas in terms of plot or characters, or does it break the rules?

c. Series: Is the book part of a series? First in a series? Must the other books in the series be read before this book, or does it stand alone?

Based on the ending, how eager are readers going to be for the next one?

d. Author: Who is the author? What else has the author written? Does the author usually write in this genre, or is this a new direction for the writer? Is this book a return to a subject the author hasn't written about for several years?

8. Using all the information gathered in the preceding questions, connect this book to other books.

   a. What genre or subgenre might this book fit in?
   b. What other books or authors share similar appeal factors?
   c. What kind of reader might enjoy this book?

When you finish, organize all your notes in a reading log or a book journal or even an online book social networking site so that you not only remember your ten-minute books but have a way to review everything you've read. The more you practice reading a book in ten minutes, the easier the process will become. One way to get better is to set a goal, such as reading a book in ten minutes once every week or reading five books in a genre you don't usually read. Any of the ideas suggested in chapter 5 of this book for professional development and genre studies can be adapted for ten-minute book reading. Once you get in the habit of reading books in ten minutes, you can easily and quickly expand your book and author knowledge and learn about many more books than you ever could just by regular reading.

Notes

1. Lisa Sampley, "How to Read a Book in Five Minutes," *Missouri Library World* 3 (Fall 1998): 33–34.

2. Joyce Saricks, *Readers' Advisory Service in the Public Library*, 3rd ed. (Chicago: American Library Association, 2005).

How to Read a Book in Ten Minutes Worksheet

1. Look at the cover: what does it tell you about the book?

2. Read the jacket blurb or back cover or both:
   a. What does it tell you about the book?
   b. Author?
   c. Other authors' opinions?

3. Check the typeface.

4. Check the physical characteristics.

5. Read a sample.
   a. First chapter
   b. Middle section
   c. Last chapter

6. Consider the appeal factors.
   a. Pacing
   b. Frame
   c. Story line
   d. Characterization

7. Consider other factors.
   a. Plot
   b. Genre
   c. Series
   d. Author

8. Connect to other books.

2

NONFICTION SPEED DATING

Sarah Statz Cords

We all know the feeling. You look across the room, and something catches your eye: a flash of color, the promise of an interesting story, the feeling that the two of you just might have something in common. So you cross that room, and you make your move . . . to pick up that new and alluring book from its spot on the display table.

It may seem strange to describe the first encounter with a new book in terms of a new romance or possibility for love. But isn't that how readers pick up books? Go anywhere books are displayed and you'll feel that same sense of delicious anticipation, that unspoken question: "Will you be the one for me?" Every time we pick up a book we feel it could be the beginning of a beautiful friendship. It's important to remember that we can feel that way not only about fiction and novels but about nonfiction as well. But for anyone more knowledgeable about and more interested in novels, it can seem a daunting task to "get to know" nonfiction, both as individual books and as a larger collection. Getting to know specific nonfiction titles as well as their place in a larger nonfiction and library collection can relieve a lot of uncertainty about working with nonfiction books and readers, and can even lead to new relationships; for this reason, I call this course of action "nonfiction speed dating."

FIRST IMPRESSIONS: THE COVER AND THE TITLE

As superficial as it may sound, a large part of the appeal of any book is its cover, and nonfiction books are no exception. Pick up a specific nonfiction book and closely inspect its cover. Don't be afraid to form those first impressions—you can always change them, and first impressions, intense as they are, are easy to remember and can help you quickly evoke feelings and perceptions about both titles and genres. Cover art is meant not only to be alluring to possible readers but also to help you ascertain a book's genre, subject matter, and sometimes even tone. Covers that prominently feature photographs or illustrations of people or groups of people are often autobiographies or biographies—in short, books in which the people are the story. The types of photographs used also provide a valuable clue; celebrity bios of well-known stars tend to feature glossy and glamorous shots, while more scholarly tomes about less notorious individuals combine portraits with other photographs or illustrations and tend to be slightly more muted in color. Some other types of nonfiction books known for their covers are business, self-help, and political titles, the covers of which often consist solely of headshots of their authors (think Jim Cramer, Dr. Phil McGraw, Ann Coulter, or Keith Olbermann). And the personal touch is not limited to portraits of people—remember John Grogan's *Marley and Me*, featuring a picture of Marley looking right at you with his gorgeous liquid dog eyes?

Of course nonfiction book covers are infinite in their variety, but when you start to study them, you'll be surprised how closely they conform to certain conventions. Memoirs, while often as personal as, if not more so than, biographies, will often feature less obvious photographs or illustrations, meant more to evoke tone and mood than to showcase the person being described. Augusten Burroughs's best-selling *Running with Scissors* is a prime example: sepia in tone, rather disturbing in its imagery of a small child with a box over his head, the cover sets the perfect unsettled mood for what is a truly disquieting family story. Books in which setting and location play key roles—environmental titles or travel books, say—will often show that location on the cover (think Frances Mayes's Tuscany books).

And of course, one of the most important things to learn about a nonfiction book can be found on its cover: the title. Unlike novel and fiction titles that can often be obscure or more ethereal in nature (Who is *The Kite Runner*? Is *Water for Elephants* primarily about elephants?), nonfiction titles are often wonders of description, efficiency, and occasional wit. Even when nonfiction titles are meant to be punchy, short, or thrilling (*Alive!*; *The Perfect Storm*; *Freakonomics*), the intrepid reader can always depend on those beautiful things, their subtitles, for the real story: *The Story of the Andes Survivors*; *A True Story of Men against the Sea*; *A Rogue Economist Explores the Hidden Side of Everything*. There's nothing coy about nonfiction book titles. They may try to woo you with an exciting or clever title

(*Blink*), but they'll always tell you all about themselves in their subtitles (*The Power of Thinking without Thinking*).

"ALLOW ME TO INTRODUCE . . .": BLURBS AND DUST JACKET COPY

Whoa, hold on there. We're not ready to do anything crazy like open that book yet. After you've mined the front cover for subject, genre, and tone clues, the time has come to turn it over in your hands and see what the back cover has to offer. More specifically, it's time to see who's recommending the book you're holding: I'm talking about those "blurbs" that authors and publishers solicit from other authors to help sell their books. I've heard these complimentary phrases derided many times, with many people feeling that they're simply purchased advertisements, but I'm a huge believer in blurbs. For one thing, authors and publishers are very interested in selling their own books, and they've been doing it for a long time—they know that readers often put a lot of stock in the opinions and words of other authors they've enjoyed. In a way, they've also done the readers' advisory work for you; when I'm stumped for read-alikes for history titles by Stephen Ambrose, for example, I'll always try to track down some of his books and see which other historians provided blurbs on his books. I should clarify that I don't often read the *text* of the blurbs—I've only got so much time and I know they're going to be positive if they're printed there—but I do love seeing which other authors are represented.

Other important parts of the jacket, of course, are the inside front flap, which you should always read, as it will nicely nutshell the book's subject and focus for you (learn to focus on valuable words and phrases like "quickly paced," "suspenseful," "comprehensive," "scholarly," "definitive," "evocative," "meticulously researched," etc.), and the back flap, which will often provide a paragraph about the author and his or her other titles.

Now—and only now—should you take the plunge and open the book.

THAT FIRST CONVERSATION: INTRODUCTIONS, PROLOGUES, TEXT, AND OTHER CLUES

One of my very favorite attributes of nonfiction books is that so many of them include introductions. Book introductions (and last chapters or conclusions) are largely what got me through college, because so much great and telling information is packed into introductions that you almost don't have to read the rest of the book (unless, of course, you want to, which I almost always do). Introductions are particularly helpful in books of history, investigative journalism, and more subject-based books such as business and political titles, as they can provide a lot of information not only about the story but about how the author will tell the story. If the introduction is long, skip to the last few pages before the first chapter starts: that's often where authors will lay all their cards on the table and explain how they wrote about their subject and what structure their books will follow. Introductions can also provide valuable clues about the narration of a book: nonfiction authors who are giving their readers the inside or hidden stories often adopt first-person and highly personal tones, promising that secrets will be revealed, while authors relying less on personal experience will adopt a more formal tone and structure. Not all nonfiction titles offer introductions, and when they don't, they might offer a prologue instead. This is particularly true in more emotion-driven works, or titles in which literary style is more of a concern than the story or characters—prologues can therefore often be found in memoirs, true crime, true adventure, and histories that are told more as stories than as scholarly works. Introductions let readers know what they're in for; prologues provide only enough information or atmosphere to tantalize.

If I've gotten this far in my cursory perusal of a nonfiction book, I've already amassed quite a bit of information. At this point I like to step back just a bit from the process and simply absorb the feel of the book. How thick is it? How heavy is it? I like to just flip through the pages as I heft it, not really reading anything but just considering little factors like the density of text, the length of chapters, whether or not there are illustrations or photo sections (which I always, always, always look through in their entirety at this point), and whether or not there are other sections like charts, appendices, notes, bibliographies, or indexes. Without considering each of those things too carefully individually, taken as an aggregate, they can provide other important clues about a book and, more important, about the types of readers who might consider picking the book up. All books, including novels, can offer wide variations in text size and spacing, depending not only on the genre but also on where the author is in her or his writing career (my husband jokes that Robert Parker's Spenser novels, while still a lot of fun to read, now feature more white space than text), but text size and spacing in nonfiction books are good indicators of the reading experience. A memoir with short chapters and more generously spaced or larger text will read much differently than will history, science, or even biographical books with denser text. Again, all these surface attri-butes will tell you much more about how a nonfiction book will "read" than will its subject classification number or interest category. Popular science books, written for a wider audience, will read much differently than will hard or more detailed science books featuring denser text, more references, or even scientific notations, numbers, or illustrations. When deciding between two such books, the popular science book might well have more in common with other, more recreational nonfiction (popular history, say, or more investigative or current affairs books) than it does with the similarly subjected hard science book.

The presence of notes or references, bibliographies, suggestions for "further reading," chronologies or time lines, or indexes can also offer you more information about the book you're holding. Books with a long list of references and an index may indicate a more scholarly or challenging read, while many new nonfiction titles are being published without any refer-ences or indexes at all (this is seen increasingly in works of popular history and biographies). Titles such as Leslie Carroll's *Royal Affairs: A Lusty Romp through the Extramarital Adventures That Rocked the British Monarchy*, with neither index nor notes, are becoming more common and are meant to be read recreationally, not studied or plundered for research projects or book reports. The presence (or absence) of notes or an index can be particularly instructive in nonfiction books written in an investigative style: exposés and works of reporting undertaken by more independent journalists will often feature more endnotes and indexes, while current affairs books by pundits and more opinionated volumes will not (references are hardly ever offered in books by authors such as Bill O'Reilly or Michael Moore).

CONTINUING THE CONVERSATION: LAST CONSIDERATIONS

If you've made it this far, you probably already have a pretty good feel for the nonfiction book you're getting to know. You could make an informed decision about this book's suitability for you (or for other readers you know) based on what you have. But if the bell hasn't yet rung and you're still en-joying yourself getting to know the book, there are just a few last things you can do, and they should largely be dictated by your personal tastes.

Although you've already had a good look at the book's introduction or prologue, you may also want to read a bit of the first chapter, or ran-domly choose a point in the book at which you'd like to start reading, just to get a better feel for the author's writing style. If I do read a bit in the book, I tend to do something that makes fiction readers very uneasy: I'll often flip right to the back and see what is in the final chapter. To each her own. For the most part, if I've had a good look at the dust jacket description and the first few pages, I don't really need to know any more to make my choice. But some readers and advisors swear by a more careful look into the middle of the book or simply reading a couple of pages at random, and I'm certainly not going to pooh-pooh that. We all get to know our books in our own ways, after all.

One thing I will do, if I have time, is peruse the author's acknowledgments, which can appear in either the very front or the very back of the book. Not only can these acknowledgments be quite heartwarming (I always like to see long-suffering family members get thanked), but sometimes I can pick up clues about other, similar books or about the author's connections. New authors will often thank or mention their authorial influences or mentors, many of whom have written books of their own—and those names can be a valuable source of read-alikes. Likewise, sometimes you can pick up a fun bit of trivia or find out why a book may suddenly and inexplicably have more "buzz" than you might expect—John Elder Robison's memoir, *Look Me in the Eye: My Life with Asperger's,* was an interesting book in its own right (with a fantastic cover, please note), but was also buzzed about because Robison is the brother of the more well-known memoirist and humorist Augusten Burroughs. I'm not even sure Robison thanked Burroughs in his acknowledgments, but that is just the sort of tangential but arguably valuable type of information that can be found amid the many thank-yous and I-owe-yous.

THE COLLECTION: THE NONFICTION BOOK AMONG ITS FRIENDS

Sometimes you're looking less for that one special book than for an opportunity to get out and mingle among a wide variety of nonfiction titles. It's possible to get to know nonfiction not only one title at a time but also as part of your larger collection. When is the last time you wandered in your stacks? How do your nonfiction shelves differ from your fiction shelves? How is your nonfiction organized, and how does that organization differ from your fiction collection? Does your library use nonfiction books in your book and other merchandising displays? All these factors will affect how you approach nonfiction books.

Because nonfiction varies so widely, from the purely informational to the more narrative, there is often a wide variation in the physical format of nonfiction books. In the nonfiction collection, books that are closer in size and shape to the vast majority of hardcover novels and fiction often have to vie for shelf space with larger and heavier coffee-table books or other oversized manuscripts as well as with much thinner how-to guides and other smaller-format informational titles. This variation in physical formats often means that the nonfiction shelves can be a bit messier and harder to browse. Don't let the chaos get to you, and embrace nonfiction's diversity. Many of those oversized books that just don't fit on library shelves are gorgeously illustrated coffee-table books on subjects that might pique your interest in more story-driven nonfiction titles. An oversized book of photographs of small-town America might get you in the mood for related nonfiction titles like Michael Perry's *Population: 485: Meeting Your Neighbors One Siren at a Time* or even novels like Richard Russo's *Nobody's Fool*.

Another particularly valuable way to explore your collection is to immerse yourself in a subject area or Dewey number range in which you have absolutely no interest. For me, a wander through the science shelves (also known as the 500s) surprisingly yielded some of my all-time favorite reads, including Matthew Hart's *Diamond: A Journey to the Heart of an Obsession*. In addition to broadening your own perspective, browsing subject areas with which you are not familiar might help jog your memory when working with science book readers or even when answering reference questions or helping patrons with their homework. By seeing beyond subject matter you will start naturally to view nonfiction as a more intangible reading experience and one more similar to the fiction experience. Although subjects sometimes do act as entry points for readers seeking novels, more often the subject matter is not as important in fiction as are appeal factors such as complex characters, evocatively described settings, or avant-garde or unique writing styles.

DID YOU MAKE A LOVE MATCH?

Even if you didn't find the book of your dreams, never fear: new nonfiction books are being published every day. There's a ton of fish in the sea—chances are good that someday you'll meet a nonfiction book you'd like to get to know a little better. In the meantime, don't forget to get out there where books congregate and make yourself available, and keep in mind the best ways to get to know nonfiction books:

- covers and titles
- author blurbs and dust jacket synopses
- introductions and prologues
- size and weight, text density, notes and references, pictures and indexes
- random chapters and acknowledgments
- subject matter and placement in a larger nonfiction collection

Happy nonfiction hunting!

See the next page for a worksheet that highlights the steps in the chapter and gives you some space for note taking. It's important to write some notes so you can remember the book you just spent time learning about. These sheets can also be saved in a binder at the service desk for moments when your memory needs nudging.

Nonfiction Speed Dating Worksheet

Title: _____

Author(s): _____

Steps (for each of these you can add a sentence or two or phrases or reminder words):

1. *First impressions: the cover and the title.* What color is the cover, and does it include photos or an illustration? Make a note of both the title *and* subtitle.

2. *Allow me to introduce: blurbs and dust jacket copy.* Who else has liked this book? Note summary and author's credentials on dust jacket copy.

3. *That first conversation: introductions, prologues, text, and other clues.* Browse the index for a summary of the story and the structure of the book. What scene does the prologue set? Are there notes, references, or an index?

4. *Continuing the conversation: last considerations.* Note literary style by browsing text; read acknowledgments for background info and possible read-alikes.

5. *The collection: the nonfiction book among its friends.* Note the shapes, sizes, and weights of books; immerse yourself in subjects.

6. *Did you make a love match?* What about it? Do you want to read this book?

3

HOW TO LISTEN TO A BOOK IN THIRTY MINUTES

Kaite Mediatore Stover

The precursor to the following guidelines, "How to Read a Book in Five Minutes," has many mothers, including the late Jane Hirsch, of the Montgomery County (Maryland) Department of Public Libraries, who developed the original guidelines. Lisa Sampley, of the Springfield–Greene County (Missouri) Library, expanded the guidelines and published them in *Missouri Library World*.[1] Further modifications have been made by Mary K. Chelton and Joyce Saricks, and Jessica Moyer has written the latest version in chapter 1 of this book.

These guidelines are suitable for books on cassettes, compact discs, Playaways, and digital audio. Unlike printed material, audiobooks are much more difficult to "judge by their covers." The narrator of an audiobook can be the sole deciding factor for a library patron. It is this quality of "listenability" that the evaluator should hone in on. The character and plot information can be gleaned from perusing the printed copy of the title. The audible qualities—narration and pacing and character voices—are of primary concern when engaging in this readers' advisory exercise.

HOW TO LISTEN TO AN AUDIOBOOK IN SIX STEPS

Tools needed: an audiobook, a listening device, a notebook or other place to jot down notes

1. *Examine the audio cover:* For cassettes, CDs, and Playaways, start by reviewing the cover. It's hard to look at the "cover" of a downloadable audiobook, but it is possible to view the online record, which usually includes an image either of the book jacket or of the audio cover.

   a. Is the cover or image attractive?

    b. Does it give the viewer a suggestion about the contents?

    c. Is it the same as the print version of the book?

    d. Is the narrator's name prominently displayed?

    e. Does the case/website clearly state whether the audiobook is abridged or unabridged?

2. *Read the jacket blurb:* Unlike on a print book, there is only one place for an audiobook blurb—the back of the case. This isn't very much room, and the blurb may be short. Again, use the record for digital audiobooks.

    a. If the print version of the book is available, peruse the flyleaf.

    b. Look for a description of the book and a profile of the narrator.

    c. Who is the narrator? Are previous works listed?

    d. Are any "extras" listed (e.g., author interviews, music, sound effects)?

    e. Do you get a sense of the story?

    f. Are key elements of the plot revealed?

    g. Can a fiction type be assigned based on the blurb?

    h. If it is a digital audiobook, editorial and listener reviews may be included. Don't forget to read these; they can be quite informative.

3. *Determine the length:* Consider the length of the recorded book. Tapes are approximately ninety minutes long, and CDs, seventy minutes. Downloads are usually six hours or less per section.

    a. How many tapes or CDs are included? If the audiobook is digital, how many parts must be downloaded?

    b. Approximately how many hours of listening time will be required?

    c. Are the tapes/CDs clearly marked on at least one side?

    d. Does the amount of listening time correspond to the abridged or unabridged formats? If you are not sure, compare the size of the book to the length of the audio. Even the shortest adult mysteries are usually at least four to five hours in their unabridged format.

4. *Listen to selections from the audiobook.*

    a. Start with the first chapter (ten to fifteen minutes, or three to four CD tracks).

        i. Does the narrator immediately start reading the story, or is there promotional, copyright, or informative material to listen to first?

        ii. Does the narrator hook the listener immediately, or does the listener need time to get into the story?

        iii. How quickly does the narrator read?

        iv. Is the pace too slow or too fast for the type of story?

        v. Is the narrator doing more narration or performance?

        vi. How well does the narrator distinguish between characters?

        vii. Does the narrator use accents or unusual vocal inflections?

  b. Skip to another tape/CD/track/section in the audiobook and listen for any irregularities in the story.

  c. Listen to portions of the last tape/CD/track/section.

        i. Is the reader's voice still recognizable and full of energy?

        ii. Is it easy to follow character changes?

        iii. Does the story still flow?

        iv. Does it appear to mesh with the book description on the back of the case?

5. *Look for extras:* Is there any music or are there sound effects?

  a. Is there special music or are there sound effects for the beginning or end of the audiobook or for both? Does the music "set the scene" or add to the listening experience or both?

  b. How is the end of a tape/CD or chapter signaled to the listener—with music or a straightforward announcement, or are there no audible cues?

  c. Are any recommendations made at the end of the audiobook?

  d. Are samples provided?

6. *Evaluate appeal, audibility, and narrator.*

  a. Is the book a good listen or a better read?

  b. If the book was abridged, did you feel as if something was missing?

  c. Who was the narrator? What other books has this person read?

  d. Who are the potential listeners?

  e. What other audiobooks have a similar listening experience?

  f. What kind of display might this audiobook be used in?

SELECTED WEBSITES FOR AUDIOBOOKS READERS' ADVISORY

Audible, Inc. www.audible.com. A subsidiary of Amazon.com, Audible is a subscription service and the leading provider of spoken audio materials (books, newspapers, magazines, original work, radio and television programming). Works with Apple and Microsoft programs. Also available for use on Amazon Kindle.

AudioFile Magazine. www.audiofilemagazine.com. The only print and electronic resource devoted to profiling the audiobook industry and reviewing audiobooks for professionals and consumers. Exceptional productions are denoted with Earphones Awards, and outstanding narrators with Golden Voice Awards.

Audio Publishers Association (APA). www.audiopub.org. The only trade association dedicated to the audiobook industry, APA gathers audiobook publishers, voice talent, retailers, suppliers, other industry professionals who are not voice talent, librarians, and media. APA bestows the Audie, a prestigious award recognizing excellence in audiobook and spoken word productions.

Grammy Award Winners. www.grammy.com/GRAMMY_Awards/Winners/. The professional association of the recording industry, music, and spoken word. Primary emphasis is on musical recordings. Grammy Awards are given in two audio categories, Spoken Word and Comedy.

ELECTRONIC MAILING LIST

audiobooks@hslc.org. Send standard subscription notice to listserv@shrsys.hslc.org.

PRINT RESOURCES FOR AUDIOBOOK READERS' ADVISORY

Books Out Loud: Bowker's Guide to Audio Books. R. R. Bowker, 2008. $345.

Whitten, Robin F. *AudioBooks on the Go.* Castine, ME: Country Roads Press, 1995. Out of print, but still valuable.

NOTE

1. Lisa Sampley, "How to Read a Book in Five Minutes," *Missouri Library World* 3 (Fall 1998): 33–34.

4

HOW TO READ A GRAPHIC NOVEL IN FIVE MINUTES

Erin Downey Howerton

If you are not already an avid reader of graphic novels, here's a quick and painless way to delve into that collection and emerge confident. Being able to enthusiastically promote your graphic novel collection will round out your readers' advisory skills and help you discover a whole new format in which you can enjoy stories. Graphic novels can be badly misunderstood by many potential readers, from the adjective "graphic" (which some believe describes the content of the story instead of the format) to the perception that they're mere comic books for kiddies. When skillfully executed, a graphic novel can be just as powerful and literary as any novel written only in text.

I happily bought into these misconceptions as a new librarian, believing graphic novels to be the sole province of people incapable of enjoying a well-written story. They must have poor reading skills, I thought, if pictures were the only way they could enjoy a book. The huge popularity of manga also turned me off. I did not particularly enjoy the artistic style of manga or anime, and I found the story lines of series like Rumiko Takahashi's *Ranma ½* to be strange and uninteresting. In my mind, everything graphic was superheroes (for little kids!) or manga (for weirdos!), and I shut myself off to their possibilities.

The graphic novel that finally proved me wrong was Gene Luen Yang's Printz Award–winning *American Born Chinese*. When it won the award in January 2007, I was very confused. How could a graphic novel have been the most "literary work" of the year? So, like any dedicated librarian, I set out to buy a copy for the flight home. I sat down in a nearby bookshop (the First Second booth having been ravaged and promptly bought out) to flip through my new copy and eat a little breakfast . . . and ended up reading the entire thing at once, then again and again on the way home.

All the value of storytelling via graphic novels suddenly became apparent to me. I simply could not imagine the story being written in a better or more skillful way than through the graphic medium. Jin, Danny, and the Monkey King were characters I could root for, and through careful rereading I was able to start seeing the visual equivalents of my favorite literary devices. The experience of being found by the right book at the right time was a rush. Now I had to make up for lost time—and dig through our graphic novel collection to see what I had previously overlooked and dismissed. What follows is my technique for getting to know a new graphic novel. Have fun reading and exploring!

PHYSICAL DIMENSIONS

Graphic novels can vary widely in size and format. Some volumes of a series might be sized like a slim, mass-market paperback while others can be quite large, printed on special papers or even heavy cardstock. The physicality of your graphic novel will often clue you in to a potential readership. For example, Craig Thompson's *Blankets* is a real tome, coming in at nearly six hundred pages. Considering it's a memoir dealing with metaphorically heavy subjects, *Blankets* will probably not be a great pick for someone reading on the go or a patron looking for a quick read.

Art Spiegelman's *In the Shadow of No Towers* is another good example of a graphic novel whose format will to some extent limit its readership. Although it is less than fifty pages long, it is an oversized book printed on very thick, almost cardboardlike pages. The hefty pages give the book a feeling of permanence and can indicate to the reader that this account of the author's life post–September 11 is a weighty work. With many books, however, size is not as obvious an indicator. The two volumes of Spiegelman's *Maus* are no bigger than many other graphic novels, but they deal with the very grave topic of the Holocaust—hardly casual reading.

The main thing to remember is that a particularly large or unwieldy book (or a tiny one, for that matter) may intimidate or turn off a potential reader. In promoting graphic novels to patrons, take the weight and dimensions of the book into consideration, because they will affect the reading experience.

COVER ART AND STYLES OF ILLUSTRATION

The cover of a book will often give you great clues about the narrative inside. You may want to take special note of the illustrations on the back cover too, as often the entire book package is carefully designed to evince the book's emotional tone and story. Yang's *American Born Chinese* cover art offers a lot to unpack—in the background is a tone-on-tone monochromatic illustration of a monkeylike character (the Monkey King) half-buried under a towering pile of rocks. In front of this landscape, a young boy (Jin) appears in full color, holding a robotic action figure. The title seems like an afterthought tacked on in the lower right-hand corner, but the careful eye will note that it mimics the style of Chinese name seals (chops). Finally, the art extends to the back cover, where we see the other half of Jin with Chin-Kee hovering menacingly over his shoulder in a television screen frame crisscrossed with grainy lines. Almost all the major characters in the novel appear on the front and back covers, and the overlapping images in the foreground and background hint at the different narrative strands of the story inside. Finally, the title itself and the use of a traditional device to illustrate it (the name chop) alludes to the very specific cultural setting in which the story is rooted: first-generation Chinese Americans.

So from only the cover art, we can deduce a lot about the events taking place in *American Born Chinese:* stories about a monkey and a boy layered over each other, traditional elements juxtaposed with a young boy who enjoys modern action figure toys, and a caricature hovering above the entire scene.

Other covers are not so obvious and set a tone and a mood rather than explicitly laying out elements of the plot. Ande Parks and Chris Samnee's *Capote in Kansas* uses only three colors: black, white, and red. The sky above a black house is blood red, and in the white light cast from its only window appears a lone figure, stepping only slightly toward the house with his back to the reader, wearing glasses and a red-and-black striped scarf. The cover uses simple shapes and a limited palette to set the mood of the narrative, in which the Clutter family is murdered and eastern dandy Truman Capote sets out to write their story. Another cover using simple shapes and elements is Marjane Satrapi's *Persepolis: The Story of a Childhood,* with a red background edged in black patterns surrounding a central blue medallion, which features a small girl. She wears a black veil over her head and shoulders and is frowning slightly at the reader with her arms crossed in front of her. Obviously, this was not a happy childhood for the main character, and we can get a feel for the story right away.

After examining the cover art, open the book and note the general style of illustration. Some readers are drawn not only to types of stories but to types of art as well. Additionally, the artistic style of the graphic novelist gives you some clues into the narrative. Are the panels or pages full of little details and screen tone/shading? Is there a lot of action and movement, or are the scenes simpler with clear, clean lines? Chiaroscuro (dramatic use of light and shadow) can indicate mystery or intrigue. Pay attention to the use of color—is the artist using full color or only selected colors? A good example of the latter is *Ghost World* by Daniel Clowes, where Enid and Rebecca's world is black and white overlaid with an aqua blue wash. Sepia tones can evoke an earlier time, as in Sfar and Guibert's *Professor's Daughter.* Sharp angles and harsh lines might suggest tension, while rounded images and softer shapes may suit a gentler story.

GENRES AND THEMES

The next thing you should determine is the genre of your graphic novel. Graphic novels are as varied as any textual novel in their genre—from non-fiction (like Jay Hosler's *Clan Apis*) to steam punk (Foglio and Foglio's *Girl Genius*), from horror (Niles and Templesmith's *30 Days of Night*) to autobiography (Alison Bechdel's *Fun Home: A Family Tragicomic*) and beyond. An excellent resource to help you recognize some of these genres is *Graphic Novels: Everything You Need to Know* by Paul Gravett. Organized around the author's own favorite graphic novels, this book has a real wealth of sample pages from major titles in the graphic novel world, allowing you to see and compare styles of illustration within specific genres.

One excellent example of a theme threaded throughout an entire novel is *The Tale of One Bad Rat* by Bryan Talbot. The title and cover are a striking homage to Beatrix Potter's *Peter Rabbit* and other tales of woodland creatures, and there are frequent references to the English author throughout. Merely glancing at the backgrounds only from start to finish, the reader will see that bleak urban scenes dominate the first half of the book, only to transition to lush panoramas of the countryside as Helen Potter, the main character, runs away to become a waitress at a village pub. In the second half of the book, she speaks to a giant imaginary rat, which is her constant companion. From the name to the settings to the illustrations and use of animals, Beatrix Potter is a guiding motif in this story about escape from an abusive childhood.

Adaptations of other stories in various mediums are fairly common in the graphics novel world. For example, the 1931 serial killer movie *M* was adapted by Jon Muth into the graphic novel of the same name. Fans of Stephen King's Dark Tower series have been eagerly enjoying the story as it is being retold in graphic novel form (David, King, and Furth's *Gunslinger Born*). Homer's tales of the Trojan War were the inspiration for the graphic novel series Age of Bronze by Eric Shanower, while traditional fairy tales are sent up in *Little Lit: Folklore and Fairy Tale Funnies,* a collection edited by Spiegelman and Mouly. Of course, one only needs to note the success of the *Batman* and *Watchmen* movies to confirm how popular movie adaptations of graphic novels can be, but these examples show that the graphic novel is a great way to plumb different depths of existing stories.

TRANSITIONS

Before and after the breaks between chapters or sections of the graphic novel, many important actions take place. Often a new character is introduced or a major incident will occur. The story line leaps forward in the transitions, and you can briefly sum up what's happened and where the story is going.

In Clowes's *Ghost World,* the transitions are often marked by Enid's appearing alone to close a section, followed by graffiti reading "ghost world" appearing somewhere in the scene to reopen the action. The phrase is written on garages, hovers over the characters like a cloud, is scribbled on windows, and appears in old photographs. It also appears repeatedly toward the end of the book, becoming a part of the story that the characters comment and act on. In this case, the transitions are also a repetition, asking the reader to make sense of recurring elements and imagery.

The Tale of One Bad Rat has only three transitions, but each helps define the story: "Town" is Helen's experience in London, trying to make a life for herself on her own. When her pet rat dies, she decides to leave town for good. "Road" does not just relate Helen's hitchhiking but also features flashbacks of Helen's life, of the metaphorical road she was on before she became homeless. The "Country" section features scenes of Helen using the physical space of the green hills to come to terms with her past and her choice to consciously become a survivor in her own story.

Parks and Samnee's *Capote in Kansas* does not feature such obvious transitions as the preceding two examples, but it can be divided into sections by full- and half-page panels that occur when the setting or the characters' point of view changes. Smaller panels indicate fast or dramatic action, with time marching quickly along, while the larger panels slow the reader down and invite a bit of contemplation before moving to the next part of the story.

READING THE PICTURES

Taking the time to quickly but methodically examine a graphic novel can not only help you get to know your collection a bit better but also help you discover appeal factors for potential readers. If you find yourself struggling, remind yourself that we are not commonly taught to decode art and images. It is a skill that you can develop and build on with practice, over time. The combination of words and pictures makes graphic novels a rich, multifaceted mode of storytelling that has a power all its own.

More than that, getting to know graphic novels will help you reach avid readers and fans as well as skeptics and those totally unfamiliar with the format. Graphic novels grow more varied and popular by the year, so *now* is always the right time to leap in and discover their power.

EXAMPLES USED IN THIS CHAPTER

Bechdel, Alison. *Fun Home: A Family Tragicomic.* Mariner Books, 2007.

Clowes, Daniel. *Ghost World.* 4th ed. Fantagraphics Books, 2001.

David, Peter, Stephen King, and Robin Furth. *The Gunslinger Born.* Marvel Comics, 2007.

Foglio, Phil, Kaja Foglio, and Brian Snoddy. *Girl Genius Volume 1: Agatha Heterodyne and The Beetleburg Clank.* Studio Foglio, 2002.

Hosler, Jay. *Clan Apis.* 2nd ed. Active Synapse, 2000.

Muth, Jon J. *M.* Abrams, 2008.

Niles, Steve, and Ben Templesmith. *30 Days of Night.* Illustrated edition. IDW Publishing, 2004.

Parks, Ande, and Chris Samnee. *Capote in Kansas.* Illustrated edition. Oni Press, 2005.

Satrapi, Marjane. *Persepolis: The Story of a Childhood.* Pantheon, 2004.

Sfar, Joann, and Emmanuel Guibert. *The Professor's Daughter.* 1st ed. First Second, 2007.

Shanower, Eric. *Age of Bronze Volume 1: A Thousand Ships.* Image Comics, 2001.

Spiegelman, Art. *In the Shadow of No Towers.* Viking, 2004.

Spiegelman, Art. *Maus I: A Survivor's Tale: My Father Bleeds History.* Later Printing. Pantheon, 1986.

Spiegelman, Art. *Maus II: A Survivor's Tale: And Here My Troubles Began.* Pantheon, 1991.

Spiegelman, Art, and Françoise Mouly. *Little Lit: Folklore and Fairy Tale Funnies.* RAW Junior/Joanna Cotler, 2000.

Takahashi, Rumiko. *Ranma ½, Volume 1.* 2nd ed. VIZ Media, 2003.

Talbot, Bryan. *The Tale of One Bad Rat.* 1st ed. Dark Horse, 1995.

Thompson, Craig. *Blankets.* Top Shelf Productions, 2003.

Yang, Gene Luen. *American Born Chinese.* Reprint. Square Fish, 2008.

PROFESSIONAL READING

Gravett, Paul. *Graphic Novels: Everything You Need to Know.* New York: Collins Design, 2005.

How to Read a Graphic Novel in Five Minutes Worksheet

Title: _____

Author(s): _____

Size: small / medium / large / other

Cover art/illustrations:

Images: Shapes/angles:

Symbols: Main character(s):

Use of color:

Genres/themes:

Adaptation   Nonfiction

Historical   Romance

Humor   Science fiction/fantasy

Memoir/autobiography   Superheroes

Mystery/horror/thriller

Allusions/metaphors:

Transitions:

Character actions: Changes in setting:

Other notes:

5

KEEPING UP
Genre Studies as Continuing Education

Lucy M. Lockley

Library staff new to the practice of readers' advisory will soon learn that the many genres of fiction and nonfiction form the basis of this popular library service. They may also be asking, "What is *genre* and why would I ever want to learn more about it?" It's also possible that they may feel comfortable with the different genres and feel they have all the knowledge they need about romance, biographies, true crime, science fiction, westerns, and the rest. For the uninitiated, *genre* refers to titles, both fiction and nonfiction, that can be grouped together by similar concepts such as subject, character, setting, plot, and theme, all of which may appeal to a particular type of reader. Understanding the differences in, and keeping current with, genre reading is an important part of any readers' advisory transaction. Studying different genres will allow both new and experienced readers' advisors to expand their personal knowledge of fiction and nonfiction and better provide readers' advisory assistance to patrons.

Suppose a public service desk staffer who is an avid mystery reader is approached by a hard-core fantasy reader asking for assistance. A working knowledge of fantasy and its elements of appeal would be very helpful for the staffer. With a little in-depth study of the fantasy genre, a readers' advisor will, at the very least, be able to tell the difference between a fantasy and a science fiction book. Having read some titles in the genre, an advisor could suggest an author or two that may interest the reader. Or, if the staffer has been involved in a library-sponsored genre study program about fantasy, coworkers who are experts in that area can be called upon for assistance.

In her book *The Romance Readers' Advisory: The Librarian's Guide to Love in the Stacks*, Ann Bouricius issues "Ann's Five-Book Challenge" to anyone interested in learning more about genre.[1] She suggests reading five books a year in one genre, especially a genre that the reader knows little or nothing about. A genre study is really just a more formal extension of this five-book idea.

According to Neal Wyatt,

> While it is inescapable that genre studies take time and energy, they pay dividends long after the last page is read and the last book is examined. There can be little better way to build RA skills and create both functional teams and a public service tone in the library than sinking into a genre for a while and working together to discover its appeal.[2]

Reading exclusively in a particular genre will not only help the readers' advisor to learn more about an individual genre as a whole but also enhance knowledge of various subgenres, authors, and publishers.

As part of this special project, library staff read and discuss individual titles representative of the genre and are encouraged to recommend these titles to others. Staff will also learn about the appeal factors of a particular genre and should be able to recognize whether a specific title is one which readers of that genre will find interesting.

A genre study will also guide staff to sources for further information, such as print tools, genre-specific awards and websites, and readers' advisory electronic discussion lists. Participants will learn quite a bit about their own reading tastes and, more important, about the areas in which they need more knowledge. Sharing this experience in a group setting will help staff members learn about the reading interests of their coworkers.

GETTING STARTED

There are a number of ways to study genres. A reader could take up Ann's Five-Book Challenge or simply begin reading about genres in any of the excellent print sources currently available. Joyce Saricks's book *The Readers' Advisory Guide to Genre Fiction* is an excellent choice for learning about genres in one volume. Choosing one of the many genre-specific titles in the Genreflecting series produced by Libraries Unlimited is another good place to start. Most of the titles in that series are expansions of either *Genreflecting: A Guide to Popular Reading Interests* or *The Real Story: A Guide to Nonfiction Reading Interests.* These two titles cover multiple fiction genres and nonfiction topics and, paired with Saricks's title, can be very useful in learning about genres individually or as part of a staff genre study.

One simple way of studying a genre would be to join a genre-specific book discussion group. Keep in mind that such a discussion group may not cover the topic with as much depth as a planned genre study simply because that may not be the group's purpose. For example, the group members may read only mysteries but might not include other aspects of the genre itself (appeal factors, reference tools, etc.) in their discussions. However, these groups can be very informative from the reader's point of view, something that is missing from most library science publications.

For a library-supported, planned genre study, start by checking with the other library systems in the surrounding area. Contact the reference staff or even the administration office and ask if any staff members have an organized genre study group. Consult with those staffers regarding setup and maintenance of a genre study program. Consider checking with the state's library association, or post a query to the association's member electronic discussion list. Don't forget about subscribing to a nationally recognized readers' advisory electronic discussion list such as Fiction_L and posing a question there.[3]

One of the best ways to become more informed about genres is to participate in or conduct an in-house genre study. If this is the preferred method, it will be helpful to answer the following questions.

WHO?

Who will participate in the genre study? A genre study could be strictly for the library's readers' advisory group or just for the professional staff. It might involve all library staff, even managers and members of the board of trustees. Some staff may need to obtain permission from supervisors in order to participate and may require an adjustment to an existing work schedule in order to attend regular meetings.

Involving staff at all levels can be instrumental in making the genre study a successful venture. Having managers and administrative staff participate in the program will allow them to see firsthand how the study is being conducted and how it can impact public service. In addition, the participants' improved readers' advisory skills should provide evidence of the genre study's being a useful, even necessary, form of staff training.

Participation by individuals other than staff may also be an option. Consider opening the genre study meetings to patrons or staff from other library systems. A project coordinator will be needed to maintain consistency and control, not to mention the schedule and readings. But rotating the leadership role will provide experience for the staff as well as draw on a pool of in-house or external reader specialists. Defining those who can participate and who will lead the genre study can help in answering many additional questions.

WHAT?

What genre or genres will be covered in the study? Most genre studies tend to concentrate on a single genre and the subgenres which comprise that topic, but the genre study can cover multiple genres. In either case, consider the order in which the various genres will be covered and develop a master schedule. That schedule will confirm consistency and should be available to the participants.

If there are members of the library staff who are considered experts in various genres, invite them to develop a presentation for the program. Perhaps there are local authors or subject experts who could talk about their writing experience or topic of interest. Often such local talent will be glad to provide training for the library staff without compensation, especially if they are well-known users of the library or members of the library's Friends group. If a book discussion format is being used for the genre study, enlist the aid of the leader of a book discussion group to conduct a genre discussion meeting.

Will the genre study include training sessions on readers' advisory tools or techniques? If the sponsoring library subscribes to online readers' advisory databases such as NoveList, Fiction Connection/Non-Fiction Connection, Books and Authors, or Reader's Advisor Online, consider some training sessions on how to use these tools. Training in various readers' advisory techniques such as how to read a book in ten minutes, how to write a review or annotation, or how to create a display could also be useful to the participants (see chapters 1, 6, or 10 of this book).

WHEN?

When will the genre study group meet and how often? Meetings can be weekly, monthly, bimonthly, or even quarterly, but it is helpful to be consistent. It is also helpful to set up a specific time of day for each session and determine, in advance, how long the meetings will last: one hour, an hour and a half, two hours, or longer. These guidelines will make it easier for participants to plan schedules and will give the leader another measure of control over the material to be covered.

How many weeks will the genre study take to complete? Some libraries set up the study as a single two- or three-hour session on the genre topic while others study a single genre for two to four months or a year. The Adult Reading Round Table (ARRT; www.arrtreads.org) in Illinois conducts in-depth genre studies that take two years to complete. The group meets every other month and covers in detail each of the individual subgenres of a particular genre. ARRT has conducted genre studies on the young adult, romance, mystery, adventure, science fiction, fantasy, and nonfiction genres. In January 2009, ARRT began a new two-year study of the romance genre. ARRT is dedicated to providing the most complete instruction possible in a genre; however, this model may not fit the schedule of most libraries.

WHERE?

Genre study meetings can be held in the same location every time, or they can rotate from branch to branch. For control purposes, the genre study leader (or someone designated by the leader) will need to book the room and notify all genre study members of the meeting place. The location and a brief description of each meeting should be included in the schedule. A disclaimer should also be included on the schedule which states that meeting locations and dates may be subject to change. If a change in location must be made at the last minute, every effort must be made to notify all members. Most participating staff will be running a tight schedule, which may include dashing back to a branch to start a public service desk shift on time.

Since 2001, St. Charles City-County Library District in Missouri has been running a continuous multigenre book discussion program that begins a new round after all genres have been covered. Round Four of the program, which began in July 2009, will take approximately four years to complete. A schedule is developed and issued, informing participants that they will meet once a month, usually in the same location, and will spend two sessions on each genre. Special training sessions on various topics take place at every fifth meeting.

WHY?

Genre studies are usually considered a form of staff training, but they are also a benefit for the staff. When developing the program, decide whether participation will be mandatory or voluntary. Another option would be to allow staff to select the sessions in which they wish to participate.

Such programs can be a form of continuing education, a means of encouraging cooperation among the staff, or a combination of both. If the genre study is set up as a form of continuing education, then participation in the program could be made mandatory for the staff. Administration may need to determine how participation in and completion of the genre study would be reflected in an individual's performance appraisal and whether staff should be compensated for the time spent in the program. Presenting a certificate of completion or offering educational credits may be another option and will certainly be a nice reward for all the work expended during the genre study.

Participation in the program at St. Charles City-County Library District is strictly voluntary, although staff members are compensated for the time spent attending a monthly meeting, which is held at a time outside a regular work schedule. The Metro Area Reader's Round Table (MARRT) in Kansas City, Missouri, has developed a Readers' Advisory Certificate that is awarded after a set number of courses has been completed.[4]

HOW?

Many genre studies use a book discussion format in which everyone reads the same title from the chosen genre or subgenre and then discusses the title at the next meeting. The schedule usually follows a pattern of announcing the selected book at one meeting and discussing it at the following meeting. In another type of format, each participant reads a different book representative of the genre being studied and then gives a brief booktalk about his or her title for the whole group at the following meeting.

Some programs study genre by using a combination of the book discussion and booktalk sessions. The selected title is announced and a date set for a discussion. At the end of the discussion meeting, the participants choose another title in the genre to read and prepare a booktalk to be given at the next meeting. With this format, every participant reads two titles in each genre but learns about a number of other titles during the booktalk session.

The genre study leader can control the program by providing a specific list of titles to choose from for the booktalk sessions, but that choice can also be left up to the individual participants. Many leaders prefer to maintain control and select titles that will be good representatives of the genre being studied. One other issue to consider is whether the participants will be provided a copy of the discussion book or will need to request a copy through the library's reserve system.

Some libraries receive a grant from the Friends of the Library group to purchase multiple copies of the discussion titles being used for each of the genre sessions. If booktalk sessions are to be conducted, then the various titles can be reserved from the library's collection by the team coordinator in advance of each meeting. The checkout period for these titles should be extended to at least one day beyond the booktalk session meeting date.

How will participants who cannot attend regular meetings be kept informed about the genre study? Set up a program-specific or general staff electronic discussion list, web page, wiki, or blog on which the coordinator can post announcements of upcoming meetings along with any materials produced for the genre study itself. This information would be extremely useful for any participant who may not be able to attend a meeting but could submit comments on a title ahead of the scheduled date. During the meeting, the leader could read those comments to the attending members and provide another point of view on the genre being studied. Obviously this method is not as good as actually attending the meeting, but it would allow external participants to convey their thoughts and comments to the group.

Any materials produced as a result of the genre study should be collected, compiled, and made available for everyone to use. The proceedings of each meeting should be recorded and reproduced as minutes, and handouts may also be produced and distributed for the participants. The participants may be asked (or required) to write a review of each book they read. At minimum, these documents could be copied and put into a binder that might be kept at the circulation or reference desk for staff to consult when performing readers' advisory transactions. Such material could also be compiled into a database and posted on the library's web page as an additional readers' advisory resource.

Other Web 2.0 technologies such as a blog or a wiki might be used to maintain a continuous record of the genre study. Consider having a specialist set up this technology and maintain it throughout the genre study. Unless staff members are expected to learn how to use these Web 2.0 technologies on their own, provide training for the genre study participants ahead of time to encourage their full and continued cooperation in the program.

Using Web 2.0 tools, the leader can post updates or relevant materials to be used at any time. The participants can add their own comments or materials any time during the full course of the study. Online access to the genre study materials can be provided for the duration of the study and even after the study has been completed. The results of the study can be compiled online, posted for further review, and used in planning future genre studies.

WRAPPING UP

So, why should a library organize a genre study? First and foremost, to expand staff knowledge of authors, titles, publishers, and appeal factors related to a specific genre. Second, to learn various readers' advisory tools and techniques. And, finally, to help library staff members to understand their own reading tastes better and get to know the reading interests of their coworkers. Studying genre as a whole will allow all staff to become more proficient in working with patrons while enhancing the readers' advisory services being provided by the library.

NOTES

1. Ann Bouricius, *The Romance Readers' Advisory: The Librarian's Guide to Love in the Stacks* (Chicago: American Library Association, 2000).
2. Neal Wyatt, "Keeping Up with Genres," *Library Journal* (November 1, 2008): 30–33.
3. Morton Grove (Illinois) Public Library, Fiction_L electronic mailing list, www .webrary.org/RS/FLmenu.html.
4. Kansas City Metropolitan Library, Metro Area Reader's Round Table, http:// kcmlin.org/marrt.htm.

Part 2

Reviewing and Evaluating Materials

6

REVIEWS AND ANNOTATIONS
FOR FICTION AND NONFICTION

Lynne Welch

With hundreds of books being published every month, librarians, teachers, and readers need easy-to-use tools to alert them to new releases and to help sort excellence from dreck. Collection development (purchasing new items for the collection and withdrawing outdated, incorrect, or damaged items), readers' advisory (finding the right book for each reader at the right time), and marketing efforts (creating displays, themed booklists, and read-alikes) are all easier to perform with the help of the two specific tools known as annotations and reviews.

ANNOTATIONS

The annotation forms the basis for reviews, booklists, and read-alikes. It is a very brief, often one-sentence, descriptive summary using strong verbs, adjectives, and adverbs. Generally limited to between thirty-five and fifty words, the annotation provides a factual identification of the genre and characters and a plot summary. Themed booklists and author read-alikes include annotations, allowing the reader to decide which of the items listed may be most intriguing based on character and plot summary, rather than merely relying on a catchy title or the author's name to spark interest. When writing an annotation, do not feel compelled to follow the usual grammatical constructions; run-on sentences composed of numerous dependent clauses are the norm.

At the end of this chapter is a worksheet useful in the construction of annotations. The worksheet is based on two brief examinations of the subject: Dorothy M. Broderick's classic article "How to Write a Fiction Annotation," originally published in *VOYA* in 1993, and Mary K. Chelton's subsequent adaptation.[1]

Joyce Saricks, in *Readers' Advisory Service in the Public Library,* articulates the elements that define and describe a particular book's appeal to readers:

- pacing (how fast does the action move along?)
- characterization (who are the characters, and how does the reader relate to them?)
- story line (the plot summary, but also whether the story is focused more on the interior landscape—the characters' thoughts and feelings—or on the exterior, with lots of physical movement and action/adventure)
- frame (the setting, both time and place, as well as the tone of the story—is it bleak and forbidding, or lighthearted and fun?—and the level of detail, whether minimal or lushly descriptive)[2]

Another aspect of frame as an appeal element relates to the author's style or voice. Does the book rely on a casual conversational style or a great deal of dialogue to advance the story line, or is the language more formal, even poetic in word choice and use? The consideration of author voice relates equally to works of fiction and of nonfiction and may be even more relevant when selecting a nonfiction title. An author's writing style can make even the most academic subject accessible and entertaining for his or her audience. Neal Wyatt specifically examines this issue in *The Readers' Advisory Guide to Nonfiction,* offering an innovative whole-collection approach to the topic.[3]

A list of questions addressing each of these appeal factors is provided both in Saricks's book and online at the Adult Reading Round Table (ARRT) Genre Study page (www.arrtreads.org/genrestudy.htm). Both of these resources also offer specific examples of the terminology commonly used to describe each aspect that may appeal to readers. For example, the ARRT Frame/Background section offers descriptors such as *bleak, contemporary, edgy, evocative, gritty, heartwarming, magical,* and many more.

With practice, identifying these elements becomes second nature. Once you have mastered "How to Read a Book in Ten Minutes" as described in chapter 1 of this book, you will be able to rapidly gauge any book, whether you have read it or not, in order to annotate it. Annotations may be verbal as well as written. You will be amazed the first time you hear yourself sum up an item's attractions during informal conversation with a reader. Listen to the way you describe how fast-paced or lushly descriptive a book may be and the title recommendations that spring forth. The verbal summary may not be as polished as the formal written annotation, but you will be able to convey the essence of the book's appeal and provide a useful service to readers as everyone works together to find the right book to read next. As an added benefit, practice in writing summaries makes it easier to use them in conversations with readers.

REVIEWS

A review is one person's opinion of the quality and appeal elements of a specific book, article, or other creative product. Reviews are written to either entice people to sample the item under review or alert them to the various reasons why the reviewer did not consider the book a worthy effort. When reading reviews, remember that every review is subjective and dependent on a number of factors, including the reviewer's frame of mind while reading the book and crafting the review. This is why reviews of the same title occasionally vary and may even seem to have been written about entirely different works!

A good reviewer, however, should always attempt to be impartial and judge the work on its merits. It is also important to write with the audience in mind. Reviews posted to a blog or website and intended for the public will use different language and possibly focus on different aspects of a book than will a review written for professional publication. Some reviews are written for readers and fans of certain types of books, whereas reviews for librarians are intended for use in collection development and readers' advisory. Awareness of the review's intended audience will help in understanding the subtext of the review.

If you are interested in learning to write for publication, study a number of reviews published in your area of interest and attempt to identify how they are similar; consider word count, formatting style, and tone (are the reviews scholarly or meant for a general audience? objective or sarcastic?). Some resources provide reviewers with guidelines to follow both in judging the merits of materials submitted for review and in crafting the review. For further guidance, search the reviewing organization's website for the guidelines or contact the editor for more information.

Types of Reviews and Common Characteristics

There are several different types of reviews. In its most basic form, a review may be limited to a plot summary for works of fiction, or a summary of the major points covered in a nonfiction article or book. An evaluative or critical review, in addition to the summary, analyzes how well the item succeeds in its goal. If the item is fiction, does it comply with the tenets of its genre, and how does it compare with benchmark works in that genre? If the item is nonfiction, the author's qualifications, as well as the subject, are examined. This examination is undertaken with specific criteria in mind:

- accuracy (is the information correct?)
- authority (who wrote it and what was the purpose?)
- objectivity (is the information presented in a biased manner?)
- currency (is the information up-to-date?)
- coverage (does the material cover the topic adequately when judged in the context of the author's intended scope?)

Additionally, consider whether the work is appropriately written (accessible and understandable, with sufficient but not overwhelming language and detail) for its intended audience.

Reviews may be long or short, but certain elements are generally present in an evaluative review. First, provide the bibliographic information for possible purchase of the item. Title, author, publisher, date of publication, cost, and ISBN/ISSN/ASIN are standard, and some reviews provide the format (paperback, hardcover, electronic, etc.) and page count as well. Then offer a hook or teaser, some element highlighted to pique the reader's interest. The body of the review provides either a brief (one to two sentences) or detailed summary of the plot, depending on the requirements of the organization publishing the review. The *New York Times Book Review,* for example, generally devotes half a page or more to each review, while most *Booklist* reviews are 175 words or less.

Next, identify the genre and compare this work to others like it. ("Fans of Dan Brown's action/adventure may enjoy this fast-paced treasure hunt with international consequences.") At the same time, summarize the frame and appeal—is it contemporary, or historical, or set in the future? Does it occur in a French château on the coast, or in an urban jungle, or on a quiet suburban street in the American Midwest? Is it recommended for all audiences or only for selected ones? This last, especially for nonfiction, may be due to the complexity of the subject matter or to the way in which the subject is treated. Also for nonfiction, the book should be evaluated in light of its initial statement of scope—what the author intends to cover— and whether the author met that goal.

When reviewing genre fiction, it is also helpful to indicate how well a book fits into the genre or subgenre under which it is marketed, or whether it is, for example, a novel of a woman's life but marketed under a romance label. Readers and librarians alike will thank you for revealing these details, because each genre establishes a set of basic expectations to be met for the tale to be appreciated as an example of that genre. Although a novel might be an excellent example of one genre, if the reader expects it to follow the conventions of another genre he or she will naturally be disappointed. Another concern in genre fiction is for series status. Is this a stand-alone title or, perhaps, the first in a series? More important, is it part of a series that has already begun, so the librarian may wish to purchase and catalog earlier titles for the collection? Providing this information, including the series name and the position of this item within the series as well as any anticipated sequels, makes a review much more useful.

Certain elements are *never* present in a well-written review. The reviewer should never include spoilers (any details that, if revealed, would reduce or eliminate the level of suspense carefully crafted by the author). Generally, it is good practice to limit description of plot points to those occurring in the first third of the book. The reviewer should likewise never give away the ending. It is permissible to indicate that an ending does not conform to expectations, but the actual details should never be revealed. There is one exception: sometimes reviewers break this rule by mentioning plot points, like dead pets or graphic violence involving children, that might be particularly upsetting to some readers. This helps readers' advisors to steer those readers away from these books.

Fiction versus Nonfiction Reviews

There are several differences between fiction and nonfiction reviews. Non-fiction must be judged on the basis of accurate and current information provided within the declared scope of the work, by a recognized authority on the subject. Narrative nonfiction must also be judged on its level of readability for a general audience, while nonfiction intended for a limited audience, such as subject experts in arcane fields, may be significantly more scholarly in style.[4] A work of fiction must conform to the requirements of its genre: if this is a mystery, the murder must be solved; if fantasy, it must take place in a fantastical setting; if horror, the threatening evil must be at least temporarily overcome by story's end. Joyce Saricks offers brief descriptions of various fiction and narrative nonfiction genres, together with lists of their appeal for readers and the top authors currently writing in each, in *The Readers' Advisory Guide to Genre Fiction*.[5] In a change from the previous edition, Saricks groups the genres by adrenaline, intellectual, emotional, or landscape, while still including genre definitions, bench-mark authors, and appeal elements. Diana Herald offers similar infor-mation for fiction genres in *Genreflecting,* and Sarah Statz Cords does the same for nonfiction in *The Real Story,* both of which are available in print or as part of the Reader's Advisor Online database.[6] Another good source of this information is freely available online: the Adult Reading Round Table is composed of "librarians and library staff who are interested in developing their Readers' Advisory skills and promoting literature and reading for pleasure" (www.arrtreads.org). Anyone interested in further-ing his or her knowledge of various genres, whether a member or not, may benefit from ARRT's so-called Genre Boot Camp, which defines each genre and offers lists of its characteristics, appeal, top authors, trends, subgenres, and resources for learning more (www.arrtreads.org/bootcamp.htm).

REVIEW WRITING: LET'S PRACTICE

You'll need a book—any book—and the worksheet at the end of this chap-ter. A copy of the ARRT Genre Study list of questions and terms or one of the other sources previously listed may also be helpful. It may be easier to take notes on character names, settings, and so forth while reading, rather than waiting until you have finished the book. However, do wait until you have finished the book before trying to answer the final question, What is the overriding impression received from this work? You may even wish to set the project aside for a day or two while considering your answer.

For your first effort, choose a book in a fiction genre you enjoy. Because you will already be familiar with the conventions and popular authors, you'll have a basis for comparison. Also, commonly accepted reviewer ethics require you to actually *read* the book you are reviewing. Annota-tions, as brief summaries without critical analysis of the merits of the item, are not subject to this requirement. While you are learning the skill, you may as well enjoy it!

After reading the book, ask yourself these questions:

What is the main focus? Is there a conflict between two characters, or between a character and a mighty but heartless and unjust organization? Is the conflict external to the characters or internal (focused on feelings, psychology, or philosophy, for example)?

Is this a character-driven story, or is the action of the plot more important? A character-driven story focuses on people: their

REVIEWS AND ANNOTATIONS FOR FICTION AND NONFICTION

emotional growth and how they react. A plot-driven story, by contrast, is more concerned with the events.

From what point of view is the story told? Is it third person, narrated by an unknown and impartial observer, or does one of the characters narrate his or her own story? How does this narrative choice contribute to the reader's sense of being part of the action or of being distant from it?

Does the story move along quickly or at a more leisurely pace? Are descriptive passages brief or detailed? Does the author use dialogue and brief sentences/paragraphs/chapters, which can enhance the reader's perception of urgency?

What is the setting, and how integral is it to the story being told? In other words, while some authors are justly famed for the quality of their research and the historical detail they incorporate into each tale, others use a particular time as window-dressing or what reviewers refer to as "wallpaper," scattering a few generalizations about the story rather than attempting to ensure that all details are properly researched and would fit within that frame. This is not necessarily a bad thing, but it is something of which the reviewer and his or her audience should be aware.

Does the author use particular stylistic devices to good account, such as flashbacks, multiple plotlines involving supporting characters, and alternating points of view? Or do these elements detract from the story line by cluttering it up and confusing the reader?

All these questions work together to provide an overall evaluation of the book and help clarify initial impressions into an opinion to share.

Referring to your notes, start by constructing the annotation. Remember to use strong verbs and feel free to pile on the adverbs and adjectives. Don't worry if your first few efforts seem awkward; this is a skill that requires practice and a willingness to break the grammatical rules drilled into us all by English teachers! Next, to transform the annotation into a brief review, break your one very long run-on sentence into its component parts and make them grammatically correct. Add your evaluation of the book's overall worthiness, suggest read-alikes or comparisons, and there you have it—your first review!

NOTES

1. Dorothy M. Broderick, "How to Write a Fiction Annotation," *Voice of Youth Advocates* (February 1993): 333; Mary K. Chelton, "How to Write a Readers Annotation," www.sjrlc.org/RAhandouts/annotation.htm.

2. Joyce Saricks, *Readers' Advisory Service in the Public Library*, 3rd ed. (Chicago: American Library Association, 2005), 40–73.

3. Neal Wyatt, *The Readers' Advisory Guide to Nonfiction* (Chicago: American Library Association, 2007).

4. Some excellent treatments on the subject of writing a nonfiction book review may be found online at academic institutional websites, such as Bluegrass Community and Technical College's "How to Write a Book Review" (www.bluegrass.kctcs .edu/LCC/HIS/review.html) and Los Angeles Valley College Library's "How to Write a Book Review" (www.lavc.edu/Library/bookreview.htm).

5. Joyce Saricks, *The Readers' Advisory Guide to Genre Fiction*, 2nd ed. (Chicago: American Library Association, 2009).

6. Wayne A. Wiegand and Diana Tixier Herald, *Genreflecting: A Guide to Popular Reading Interests*, 6th ed. (Santa Barbara, CA: Libraries Unlimited, 2005); Sarah Statz Cords and Robert Burgin, *The Real Story: A Guide to Nonfiction Reading Interests* (Santa Barbara, CA: Libraries Unlimited, 2006).

Annotation Worksheet

Title: _____

Author(s): _____

Publication info:_____

Identify the central character (the protagonist) and his or her identifying characteristics (background, goals, age/race/ethnicity, etc.):

Significant other characters (which characters will most affect the protagonist?):

Setting (place and time frame):

Pacing (leisurely? rapid? densely descriptive?):

Sensuality rating/level of violence/other caveats (reading level; if nonfiction, is it for elementary/middle/high school/college?)

Most important challenge faced by the protagonist:

Roadblocks to success (what is the root of the protagonist's problem—personal characteristics, societal issues, natural disasters, etc.?):

Which of the above elements are essential to convey? Construct one sentence including these, using strong verbs, adjectives, and adverbs in thirty-five to fifty words. Avoid passive tense.

Adapted from Dorothy M. Broderick's "How to Write a Fiction Annotation" in *VOYA* (February 1993), p. 333, with permission.

7

REVIEWING AUDIOBOOKS

Sue-Ellen Beauregard

As leisure reading expands to include more technological formats, it is more important than ever to consider books in conjunction with these new formats and not simply as printed material. A book in print has the advantage of focusing solely on the author's intentions. A book in audio format adds a very crucial element to the author's finished product, one that can go beyond the author's intentions or obscure them.

Reviewing books in audio form is as important as reviewing a book in traditional form. As libraries see enormous increases in the circulation of books in varying audio formats and increase the collection development budgets for audio materials, it is imperative that library staff understand how to evaluate an audiobook, taking into consideration production values as well as book content.

Reviewing an audiobook is not the same as reviewing a printed book. We are not judging the quality of the writing (although a poorly written book rarely makes a dynamic audio), but evaluating how the book translates to audio. How do we begin to evaluate an audiobook and write a descriptive audio review? The process can be broken down into ten easy steps.

STEP ONE: LISTEN TO THE AUDIO AND TAKE NOTES

This might be the easiest step. The hard part comes later when writing the descriptive and critical review. Begin by listening to the audio and taking notes as the story progresses. It is important to take notes because it can be difficult to remember all the points to make when it comes time to write the review or annotation. Taking notes is a necessity for composing a thoughtful and critical audio review.

What qualities should the reviewer listen for? Of primary importance is the reader. Pay attention to the narration and any other audible embellishments, such as music and sound effects. In order to competently evaluate an audio recording, we'll need some criteria on which to base judgment.

STEP TWO: EVALUATE THE READER

A good place to begin an evaluation is to consider the reader or narrator. Aspects to think about (and take notes about) include vocal as well as creative elements.

Does the reader have good voice quality, diction, timing, and pacing? Is he or she believable and convincing? Mary Burkey, the chair of the 2008 Odyssey Award for Excellence in Audiobook Production committee, uses the phrase "wall of performance" to describe a good reader. Like accomplished actors, audiobook readers should come across as authentic and real. Burkey says, "The mark of an excellent audiobook lies in its ability to remove the wall of performance and draw listeners into the reading with little effort."[1] The narrator should be so natural and convincing that listeners will hardly notice the recording is a performance.

The 2009 Odyssey Award for Excellence in Audiobook Production went to Recorded Books for its production of *The Absolutely True Diary of a Part-Time Indian,* written and narrated by Sherman Alexie, whose outstanding reading was integral to the impact of the semiautobiographical novel.[2] This audio is an exception to the widely held belief that authors rarely make good readers. Why do authors often make poor readers? Primarily because they are not trained actors (as are most professional audiobook readers). Authors may try too hard to emphasize the portions of a book they feel are very important and end up overacting. Often their deliveries are too stiff and impersonal, and they may find it difficult to connect with listeners.

Pacing is another important element to watch for when reviewing an audiobook. In a mystery title, for example, the pacing may help build tension or signal changes in the story's direction. In literary novels, the reader may linger over the lyrical prose, helping draw listeners into the language.

Proper pronunciation can be crucial to an audiobook's quality. Does the reader pronounce words, including foreign phrases, geographic locales, and distinctive character names, correctly and consistently? There is nothing more cringe inducing than hearing words mispronounced. And this happens more often than expected. The mark of an excellent production is one in which there are no mispronunciations. Dictionaries and other reference sources are always at hand in the recording studio, and it is up to the production team to verify pronunciations, but too often this does not happen. Some readers (or the production team) check with the author to learn pronunciations of unusual character names. Although one mispronunciation might not be a deal breaker when evaluating an audio, if it occurs often or is blatantly overt, it is definitely worth mentioning in the review.

Accents are also important considerations (see step 7). Are they used in the reading and, if so, are they authentic and consistent? It is more realistic when the voices match the setting of the text. This is why British narrators are often used for titles with British themes and settings. Lisette Lecat, a native of South Africa, reads Alexander McCall Smith's popular No. 1 Ladies' Detective Agency series, which is set in Botswana and features beloved amateur detective Precious Ramotswe. Lecat, an accomplished audiobook reader, renders the lively lilt of all the Botswanan characters, drawing listeners into the characters and the setting. These productions are greatly enhanced by using a reader whose accents and dialects are truly authentic.

Finally, listen for how the reader distinguishes characters in a work of fiction. Is there a change in pitch, tone, and inflection to help the listener keep the characters straight? Does the narrator lighten tones to reflect the female voices and deepen a bit for the male voices? Is the production a straightforward reading with no attempt at character differentiation? Does the reader go the extra mile and create unique voices for each character, as Jim Dale does in the award-winning Harry Potter series? There is no right or wrong answer, but however the character voices are handled, they should be read in a consistent fashion. If the characterizations sound too forced or unnatural, the reading is not effective. The narrator should convey the text through engaging expression, emotion, and energy.

STEP THREE: ASSESS THE TECHNICAL QUALITIES

As noted, the reader is generally the main element noticed in a recording, but there are technical qualities worthy of attention. Is the recording marked with crisp sound and steady volume levels? The sound quality should be clear (not muddy), and the volume level should be the same throughout. Lengthy books are not recorded in one day, yet listeners should not be able to discern any differences in the narrator's voice or the points at which one recording session ended and the next began. Distracting breathing and swallowing noises, extreme sibilance, and other mouth sounds should not be apparent. The volume levels must remain constant.

If music and sound effects are used, do they enhance the text and support the vocal performance? Music has long played a part in audiobooks, cuing listeners to chapter beginnings and endings, signaling transitions, and emphasizing moments of great emotion, or even emphasizing the setting and atmosphere. In the Phryne Fisher series from Bolinda Audio, the audio opens and closes with a short selection of lively jazz music, reflecting the modish 1928–1929 setting and Phryne's flapper image. In other productions, such as Gail Carson Levine's *Fairest*, from Full Cast Audio, and Laura Amy Schlitz's *Good Masters! Sweet Ladies! Voices from a Medieval Village*, from Recorded Books, music has moved from the background to an integral part of the production. Whether it holds a supporting or starring role, the music should not overwhelm the production and should add to the overall atmosphere and mood.

If sound effects are used, they too should not overshadow the reading. Unless an audio production is a full-cast recording more in line with a play than a novel, there won't be very many sound effects present. That said, *Prodigal Summer*, from Harper Audio, written and narrated by Barbara Kingsolver, employs original birdsongs to denote the ending of chapters and transition to a new character's viewpoint. The birdsongs enhance the novel's rural Appalachian summer setting and remind listeners how important time and place are in this leisurely paced novel.

STEP FOUR: CONSIDER THE ENTIRE PRODUCTION

Think about the audiobook in its entirety. Does the audio production do justice to the book, pulling all audible and written elements together as a unified whole? Can the audio stand alone as a substitute for the book? Some books translate better to audio than others, and some audios even transcend the print version. The bottom line is that the audio should stand as a substitute for the book, allowing listeners to immerse themselves in the reading. This is a judgment call on the part of the reviewer. Take all the elements considered thus far and make a careful and considered evaluation of the audio before writing the review. The review of the printed work will serve as an excellent reminder of the book's plot and characters.

STEP FIVE: BEGIN WRITING THE REVIEW

Look over your notes, consider the important points, formulate your thoughts, and begin writing. Often the hardest part of writing is getting started. Even if the first draft is not the best effort, you will now have something to work with and rewrite. What our English teachers told us still works—begin with a topic sentence. Although the main intent of the review is to talk about the audio qualities, you also need to describe some elements of the book so that readers of the review understand what the story is about.

Grab attention with your first sentence. Here are some first sentences of audio reviews that set the stage. The review of Tina Brown's *Diana Chronicles* (from Books on Tape) begins, "Brown's blockbuster book translates well to audio."[3] The reviewer of Ellen Crosby's *Bordeaux Betrayal: A Wine Country Mystery* (from BBC/Sound Library) gets our attention with this opening sentence: "Veteran theater actress Marshall serves up a crystal-clear reading of Crosby's third wine-country mystery."[4] And the review for Mark Twain's *Adventures of Tom Sawyer* (from Blackstone Audio) has this catchy beginning: "Gardner's reading of Twain's classic convinces us why certain titles remain in the pantheon of must-reads (and must-listens)."[5] In each of these cases, the reviews go on to support the topic sentence, covering both the audio portions and plot (in the case of a novel) details. A big mistake many audiobook reviewers make is to merely recap the plot. Writing a plot summary is easy, but it does not constitute an audio review. Audio reviews must also convey the listening experience.

STEP SIX: REFLECT ON THE CRITERIA WHILE COMPOSING THE REVIEW

While formulating the review, keep in mind the criteria from steps 1, 2, and 3 and your general impressions during listening. Consider the pacing, accents, character differentiation, sound effects (if any), musical interludes, chapter breaks, and overall technical qualities. Especially consider what the narrator brings to the production and incorporate this element into a cohesive, smoothly flowing evaluative review. Use short, punchy sentences with descriptive adjectives if the review will be used for a library newsletter or a website as well as a professional review. Your goals should be to keep it simple, grab readers' attention, and maintain interest.

Joyce Saricks provides an example of an audio review that covers all the bases and makes listeners want to check out the audiobook. Saricks begins her review of Alice Sebold's *Almost Moon* (from Books on Tape and read by Joan Allen) with this attention-getter: "Sebold's second novel, following *The Lovely Bones* (2002), opens as dramatically as the first."[6] Saricks goes on to describe the plot, which follows the life of a 49-year-old seemingly normal woman who smothers her senile mother, tends to the body, and moves on with her life. Although the plot may be somewhat distasteful, the reading is an effective reflection of the murderous woman. Saricks writes,

> Allen owns this reading from the very first sentence. Her sublime narration adds a very personal, emotional level to the lyrical prose. Allen's voice seduces, probes, hesitatingly discovers, and chills, transcending mere words into disturbingly candid and haunting insights of a woman who is clearly not entirely sane. She is absolutely convincing in her first-person portrayal of Helen. Her confiding, yet frighteningly normal, tones lay open Helen's innermost thoughts and impulses, and her interpretation forces us to question how much of Helen's memories and motives can be believed. This audio presentation elevates this disturbing tale.[7]

In this case, Allen uses no accents because the novel is told in the first-person words of an American woman. But when accents are used, they should always be mentioned in the review, and that leads to the next step.

STEP SEVEN: DISCUSS ACCENTS IN THE REVIEW

Many times reviewers will discuss the reading but never mention specific dialects or accents. It is important to let readers know if accents are used in an audio production. For example, do not assume that everyone knows Jim Dale is British. In her review of *Alice's Adventures in Wonderland* (from Listening Library), Kristi Elle Jemtegaard notes that the reading is done in a British accent. Jemtegaard begins the review by stating that many classic tales have been recorded numerous times and *Alice's Adventures in Wonderland* is no exception.

> Has the Queen of Hearts' anger ever been so florid, the hookah-smoking Caterpillar's ennui so languid, the White Rabbit's nattering so fusty? . . . The fact that a mature male narrator can pull off the voice of a little girl without sounding phony or condescending is nothing short of a miracle. And even though Dale's voice is certainly well known due to his remarkable reading of the Harry Potter titles, it never gets in the way as

listeners become immersed in this timeless classic, read in his distinctive and commanding British-laced delivery.[8]

Many, if not most, audiobook fans are familiar with Dale and know that he is a British actor; however, it is still important to include that fact in the review, because not every listener and certainly not every readers' advisor will know.

In a recent review of a title in Alexander McCall Smith's engaging series featuring Edinburgh moral philosopher Isabel Dalhousie, read by London native Davina Porter, the reviewer stated, "As the voice of Isabel, Porter is perfect." The reviewer goes on to say that Porter "delivers sharply rendered narrative passages, charming and revealing character voices, and accents that place listeners deep in the landscape." Although these sentences are fine, they really don't provide specifics about Porter's reading. When reviewing, do not assume anything! Querying the reviewer about the accents, I was told that the Scottish characters spoke in Scottish accents while the rest of the narrative was read in Porter's native British accent. Be specific in descriptions and remember that most people who read the review or critique have not heard the audio. It is the job of the reviewer to discuss accents for many reasons, one of which is to help readers' advisors match listeners with appropriate audios.

STEP EIGHT: AVOID CLICHÉS AND VAGUE DESCRIPTIONS

Saying a reader "brings life to the production" really doesn't say anything at all. "Nuanced reading" is another vague description. What does that phrase really tell us about the reader? Critiquing Simon Vance's reading of Eric Clapton's memoir, *Clapton* (2007), the reviewer states, "Vance's delivery convincingly communicates the mood swings of an insecure musician, expressing palpable and perhaps overblown regrets of a life largely wasted in a haze of inebriation."[9] Now isn't that sentence much more expressive than "brings the audio to life" or "nuanced reading"? Use descriptive adjectives and be as specific as possible.

I once received the following from a reviewer: "The narrator has firmly set her dramatic compass so as to intensify and expand the author's intent. Her ability to embrace and reflect the moods, wishes, and emotions of the teenage characters is extraordinary." These sentences don't really tell us much about the narrator. If the reviewer had expounded *how* the reader embraced the moods, wishes, and emotions of the teen characters, the review would have been much stronger.

Compare the preceding sentences with a review of Philippa Gregory's *Other Queen*, narrated by Stina Nielsen, Jenny Sterlin, and Ron Keith, and available from Recorded Books:

> All three are excellent readers, especially Sterlin, whose range of emotions encompasses love, anger, jealousy, and fear, each one clearly delineated. In her commanding British tones . . . , she imitates the often-tempestuous Mary, Queen of Scots. As the Earl of Shrewsbury, Keith captures the heartsick longing for the safety of his prisoner even while she is driving him into financial ruin. It is only when she betrays his trust that his disillusionment comes through. Keith and Sterlin's dialogues and falling-outs as husband and wife are wonderfully portrayed. Mary can come across as seductive, dishonest, disingenuous, and angelic, but she is always the queen and thus somewhat condescending in tone.[10]

These sentences are specific with respect to the emotions that Jenny Sterlin reflects in her reading. The review also tells us that she speaks in "commanding British tones."

STEP NINE: USE CORRECT GRAMMAR, PUNCTUATION, AND SPELLING

As you write more and more reviews or annotations, you will find your own style and your own way of writing. But whatever your style, you must of course use proper grammar, punctuation, and spelling. I am sometimes appalled at reviewers who send in reviews that have misspellings or contain words that are not in the dictionary. Recently I received a review that used the word *ratchety* to describe a character. Is this a cross between cranky and crotchety? It is not in the dictionary. Readers of reviews or annotations expect accuracy, and although everyone makes mistakes, do the best job possible to ensure correctness in all phases of the review. Check that all proper names (authors, readers, characters) and words are spelled correctly. If unclear on any spellings or usage, consult reliable reference sources. Do not rely on the computer spell-checker. Do it the old-fashioned way—consult a print dictionary.

STEP TEN: ENJOY YOURSELF

Listening to an audiobook and critiquing the performance should not be a chore but an enjoyable endeavor. The more you do it, the easier it will become and the more qualified you will be in your ability to judge an audio production. Following the preceding steps will help you capture the essence of the audiobook in your review.

Notes

1. Mary Burkey, "Sounds Good to Me: Listening to Audiobooks with a Critical Ear," *Booklist* (June 1, 2007): 104.

2. American Library Association, Odyssey Award for Excellence in Audiobook Production, www.ala.org/ala/mgrps/divs/yalsa/booklistsawards/odyssey/odyssey.cfm.

3. Sue-Ellen Beauregard, review of *The Diana Chronicles*, by Tina Brown, narrated by Rosalyn Landor (Books on Tape, 2007), *Booklist* (September 1, 2007): 142.

4. Allison Block, review of *The Bordeaux Betrayal*, by Ellen Crosby, narrated by Christine Marshall (BBC/Sound Library, 2008), *Booklist* (December 1, 2008): 71.

5. Patricia Austin, review of *The Adventures of Tom Sawyer*, by Mark Twain, narrated by Grover Gardner (Blackstone, 2008), *Booklist* (December 1, 2008): 73.

6. Joyce Saricks, review of *The Almost Moon*, by Alice Sebold, narrated by Joan Allen (Books on Tape, 2007), *Booklist* (February 1, 2008): 62.

7. Ibid.

8. Kristi Elle Jemtegaard, review of *Alice's Adventures in Wonderland*, by Lewis Carroll, narrated by Jim Dale (Listening Library, 2008), *Booklist* (December 15, 2008): 59.

9. Mike Tribby, review of *Clapton: The Autobiography*, by Eric Clapton, narrated by Simon Vance (Books on Tape, 2007), *Booklist* (February 15, 2008): 98.

10. Mary McCay, review of *The Other Queen*, by Philippa Gregory, narrated by Stina Nielsen et al. (Recorded Books, 2008), *Booklist* (January 1, 2009): 100.

8

HOW TO REVIEW GRAPHIC
NOVELS AND MANGA

Jessica Zellers

Reviewing graphic novels and manga is not so different from reviewing traditional print books. The same elements that are important in traditional books—plot, characters, writing style, setting, pacing, and atmosphere—are important in graphic materials. One significant difference, however, is that visual elements must be considered, in the same way that narration must be considered when reviewing audiobooks.

Not to mince words, but this point is rather obvious: *of course* you must review the artwork when you review graphic materials. This element can be intimidating, though. Librarians who work with books and readers quickly learn how to discuss the written word; discussing visual art, on the other hand, is not part and parcel of the librarian skill set.

Furthermore, many librarians—even well-read librarians who enjoy a variety of fiction and nonfiction genres—are largely unfamiliar with graphic materials. Most everyone has a passing familiarity with traditional print books; even avowed nonreaders will have encountered books in school. Graphic materials, however, are not a standard part of the curriculum. Even highly educated librarians who love to read might never delve into the graphic format.

There's no cause for alarm here. Even if you aren't familiar with graphic novels and manga, the tools for reviewing graphic materials are simple to use.

WHY AND WHEN TO REVIEW GRAPHIC MATERIALS

Generally, the act of writing reviews makes for good professional development. Reading and understanding a book, and then articulating its appeal, is an excellent way to practice the skills of readers' advisory.

If your library already features book reviews (in the building, in the newsletter, online, or elsewhere), by all means include the occasional graphic novel and manga; after all, it's only fair to promote the graphic format if you're also promoting traditional books. But you don't need to review graphic materials just because of a vague sense of obligation; you can review them for three very definite purposes.

1. *Draw in reluctant readers.* A short synopsis of an engaging graphic novel, displayed in conjunction with the book or its cover art, will lure people who might not otherwise read books. Try setting up a mini-display of graphic novels and reviews in the computer area to attract tweens, teens, and young men.

2. *Draw in readers of traditional books.* Lots of people have misconceptions about the graphic novel format. It's true that some titles are fluffy, juvenile, and lowbrow, as the old stereotype suggests—but it is also true that some titles are sophisticated and complex. Graphic novels come in every genre, fiction and nonfiction alike, with something to appeal to every type of reader (even the picky ones!). Because of the artwork in graphic materials, the act of reading graphic novels and manga is somewhat different than the act of reading a print book—but it can be satisfying in exactly the same ways.

3. *Boost circulation for sluggish titles.* Most likely, the superhero books and manga series books are flying off the shelves, but stand-alone titles sometimes need extra help. Use a review to attract readers to titles that have languished on the shelves. (Incidentally, this can kill two birds with one stone: when you highlight stand-alone books, you draw those readers who had mistakenly dismissed graphic novels as being the sole province of caped crusaders.)

BEFORE YOU BEGIN: TERMINOLOGY

It is essential that you communicate as clearly as possible with your audience, but you're working with a serious handicap, as the jargon of graphic novels is frustrating and ambiguous. In this particular chapter, the phrase *graphic materials* refers to narrative stories told through the form of sequential art, but you don't want to toss that phrase around just anyplace; taken out of context, most folks will think you're talking about naughty books that are sold in discreet brown paper bags.

Graphic novel is the term most commonly used to describe works of sequential art, whether or not those works are novels. (*Sequential art* is perhaps the most accurate term available, but unfortunately, few people know what it means and even fewer people use it.) Graphic novels are not necessarily novels at all; they might be graphic nonfiction. To confuse matters further, graphic novels sections in bookstores and libraries often include books of *non*sequential art—that is, collections of discrete comic strips and single-panel cartoons.

Then there is manga, a particular type of graphic novel. Most manga comes from Japan. A close cousin to anime television shows and anime movies, manga features stylized art and usually reads from right to left. And while manga books are indeed graphic novels, the readership between the two camps of graphic novels—those that are manga, and those that are not—does not always overlap.

When writing a review, your job is to identify a book's form as clearly as possible. Use the terms that you think will best communicate with your audience, and avoid terms that will confuse them.

HOW TO REVIEW GRAPHIC NOVELS AND MANGA IN EIGHT STEPS

Tools needed: a graphic novel or a manga, materials for taking notes

1. *Read the book.* Endeavor to read it carefully. Graphic materials are faster reads than traditional print books because they contain less text, but fly through them too fast and you'll miss something.

2. *Reread or skim.* This time, focus on the art. Try to catch details you may have missed on your first reading.

3. *Identify the format.*
   a. Is the book a full-text narrative? A collection of shorter stories? A compilation of comic strips or cartoons?
   b. Is the book a manga, or is it some other type of graphic novel?
   c. Is it fiction or nonfiction? If it is nonfiction, make this distinction clear if you refer to the book as a graphic novel.

4. *Consider the interplay of art and text.* As with any book, you'll want to consider the standard appeal characteristics: story, writing style, characters, setting, pacing, and tone. But with graphic materials, you need to determine whether the art or the text is driving those characteristics.
   a. Do the art and text support each other equally, or is one more important than the other? Are vital parts of the story delivered through the art alone, or the text alone?

  b. Which appeal characteristics are developed primarily by text? By art? For example, is the tone communicated by the text, by the colors on the page, or by both?

  c. Is the book text-heavy?

  d. Do the art and text dovetail gracefully, or are there parts where they seem to contradict each other? If there are contradictions, are they deliberate or merely confusing?

5. *Consider the art in-depth.*

  a. Is the book in color or black-and-white?

  b. If there are colors, what are they like? Vibrant, bold, brilliant? Muted, understated, subdued?

  c. Are the illustrations easy to interpret and understand?

  d. Is it easy to follow the illustrations from panel to panel? Does the eye know where to go along the page?

  e. What is the style like? Clean and crisp? Realistic or impressionistic? Stylized, derivative, unusual, edgy?

6. *Look for sex, violence, and body appearance.* With any book, it's important to let readers know how sex, violence, and body image are treated, but it's especially important to discuss these aspects in graphic materials. You can choose to skip a paragraph in a traditional book; with graphic materials, the images are unavoidable, so readers deserve to know what they'll be getting before they ever crack open the book.

  a. Are human bodies shown realistically? Are there a variety of ages, races, and body weights?

  b. Are sexual features exaggerated? Are the women especially busty? Do the men sport extraordinary muscles?

  c. Are nudes drawn with close-up details, or with murky details? Are men as well as women shown without clothes?

  d. Do any characters engage in sex? If so, is it implied by the text or depicted on the page? If sex is depicted, is it with explicit detail?

  e. How is violence treated? Is it slapstick, psychological, graphic? Frequent, gory, personal, mundane?

7. *Consider culture.* If you're reviewing books for a North American audience, pay particular attention to books that hail from different cultures. This is especially true with manga books, nearly all of which come from Japan; other Asian countries—and increasingly, some European countries—are producing graphic materials that are being marketed toward North American audiences.

   a. Do foreign customs, practices, and mores influence the book? Will these influences frustrate or enlighten readers?
   b. Are minors sexualized? What is perfectly normal in one country may raise eyebrows in another. Will readers be unnerved, titillated, unaffected?
8. *Consider other elements.*

   a. What age group would the book appeal to? (Publishers often offer suggestions on the back cover.)
   b. What type of audience would the book appeal to? Crime fans, fantasy readers, literary fiction readers, nonfiction aficionados?
   c. Is background information preferred or necessary? With superhero books in particular, it can help to understand the larger story arc of the characters. Is the book satisfying even without this background?
   d. If the book is part of a series, is it necessary to read the books in series order?

Sample Review

Fullmetal Alchemist, volume one, with story and art by Hiromu Arakawa. Hiromu Arakawa, Egan Loo, and Wayne Truman. 2005. *Fullmetal alchemist, 1.* Viz graphic novel. San Francisco: Viz.

You may already be familiar with the animated television show of the same name, but *Fullmetal Alchemist* began as a manga series that is still going strong. Enter this strange universe with the first book in the series, a collection of loosely related stories about two brothers, Edward and Alphonse Elric. The action-filled stories are campy, screwball, and fun, propelled by the hijinks of the brothers as they use alchemy, the height of scientific progress in this alternate history. Our heroes transmute matter to defeat any number of bad guys, but not without a cost—older brother Edward is missing an arm and a leg, and Alphonse, though younger, is definitely bigger: having lost his human body through an alchemical experiment gone awry, his soul now resides in a giant suit of armor. Will the brothers ever regain their original forms? Not in this book—but read the series, preferably in order, to follow their quest. Though the illustrations are slightly confusing on occasion, the engaging manga style, rendered in evocative black-and-white, adds plenty of high-octane impact to the brothers' adventures. This is a great choice for tweens, teens, and anybody with a sense of fun.

SELECTED RESOURCES FOR REVIEWING GRAPHIC MATERIALS

GNLIB. Get fast, valuable answers to questions with the Graphic Novels in Libraries electronic mailing list. Sign up at www.angelfire.com/comics/gnlib/. (This is a high-traffic list, so you may wish to divert everything into one folder or to sign up for the digest format.)

Scott McCloud, *Understanding Comics: The Invisible Art* (New York: HarperTrade, 1994); *Reinventing Comics: How Imagination and Technology Are Revolutionizing an Art Form* (New York: HarperTrade, 2000); *Making Comics: Storytelling Secrets of Comics, Manga, and Graphic Novels* (New York: HarperTrade, 2006). McCloud has written three nonfiction graphic novels that, both individually and collectively, illuminate the graphic format. Good for novices and veterans alike, these informative, entertaining books explain the appeal of graphic materials. For maximum impact, read them in publication order; if you have time for only one, make it *Understanding Comics.*

Michael Pawuk, *Graphic Novels: A Genre Guide to Comic Books, Manga, and More* (Westport, CT: Libraries Unlimited, 2007). With a succinct, engaging style, Pawuk describes the appeal of the various genres of graphic novels. And the many, many reviews of graphic novels within the book provide excellent examples of how to write a good review.

No Flying, No Tights (www.noflyingnotights.com). There are many excellent, free websites of graphic novels reviews, but this one is a mainstay. Created by librarian Robin Brenner, the site posts reviews by several contributors. The reviews—arranged into age-appropriate levels—cover a variety of reading interests. Use the reviews for inspiration for writing your own reviews. Although this site has not been updated as frequently as in the past, it is still a valuable resource for librarians new to graphic novels. For more recent materials, try Graphic Novel Reporter (www.graphicnovelreporter .com).

Graphic Novel Review Worksheet

Title: _____

Series: _____

Author(s): _____

Format: _____

Plot summary: _____

Interplay of art and text:

    Do they support each other? Which has the vital parts of the story?

    Appeal characteristics in text

    Appeal characteristics in art

    Do text and art dovetail or contradict? Is it deliberate or confusing?

Art in depth:

    Colors: Vibrant, bold, brilliant? Muted, understated, subdued?

    Illustrations: Is the story line easy to follow and understand?

    Art style: Clean and crisp? Realistic or impressionistic? Stylized, derivative, unusual, edgy?

Sex, violence, and body appearance—How are they treated?

Culture:

    Do foreign customs, practices, and mores influence the book?

    Are minors sexualized?

    What is perfectly normal in one country may raise eyebrows in another. Will readers be unnerved, titillated, unaffected?

Other:

    Age group

    Type of audience—who else might like this?

    Is background information necessary to enjoy the book? Is it part of a series?

9

REVIEWING AND EVALUATING
REFERENCE MATERIALS

Jessica E. Moyer

An important part of working as a readers' advisor is evaluating and reviewing reference resources. Understanding how reference materials are reviewed makes it easier to read and understand reviews, which can be a great assistance in collection development. This chapter is not an overview of all the tools available to readers' advisors, but is, rather, a guide to evaluating tools to be used as reference resources. These guidelines will help in making purchasing decisions, in writing annotations, in promoting RA tools to library staff, and in evaluating tools when weeding reference collections.

Print, online, and subscription resources can all be important tools for readers' advisory work. In terms of evaluation these resources share similar characteristics, but there are enough differences that each will be discussed in a separate section. Print sources have been around the longest and are still going strong. The two major publishers are ALA Editions, which publishes more professional development titles like Joyce Saricks's *Readers' Advisory Service in the Public Library,* and Libraries Unlimited, which has more genre-oriented tools like its flagship book *Genreflecting* (6th ed.) and its spin-offs, such as *Fluent in Fantasy* or *Make Mine a Mystery.* But reference tools for readers' advisory are not limited to these publishers; there are plenty of others to consider. Electronic subscription-based tools for readers' advisory are gaining in importance, and new ones are introduced every year. Because these are often quite expensive, careful evaluation is essential before purchase. Nearly all the major subscription vendors have some tools that would be relevant to readers' advisory work. Last, the World Wide Web provides us with many possible tools. Here the critical issue is not price, but selection. With so many resources to choose from, and few reviewed in professional journals, librarians looking to add web-based RA tools to their professional collections or library web pages need to evaluate all possible candidates.

The next three sections will lead you through the steps of evaluating print, subscription, and web-based tools. Each section includes many questions and key issues that should be addressed in a written review. As you work through these sections, remember to take notes.

PRINT REFERENCE TOOLS

1. Get the book in hand, along with any previous editions.

2. Look at the front and back.

   a. Is there more than one volume? Is that information clearly stated on the cover?

   b. Does the title indicate whether the book is a dictionary, an encyclopedia, or something else?

   c. Is an author or editor listed? Have you heard of this person? Has he or she written other reference tools?

   d. The back cover generally includes a summary; what does it tell you about the subject area, content coverage, and types of entries? Does it say anything about the intended audience? Additional author/editor information is sometimes found here.

3. Look over the introductory materials. Read the title page, preface, and any other introductory materials. (Don't read the "how to use this book" section or the more in-depth introduction yet—that's the next step.)

   a. What additional information is provided about the author, type of work, and subject matter?

   b. Why was this particular work created?

4. Read the introduction and the "how to use this work" section. Outside of the indexes, these are the most useful and informative sections.

   a. What is the subject matter and coverage? What is and is not included? Is the book an overview or an in-depth treatment?

   b. Are there subject entries? Biographical entries? Maps or other illustrations?

   c. Are any other works mentioned as complementary or competitors? Is this a prequel or sequel?

   d. Determine if the book is a dictionary, encyclopedia, or other type of reference tool. This makes a big difference in how the work is used and how the entries are set up.

e. Additional author or editor information should be nearby—make sure to read it. Who is the author? How qualified is the author to write this work? Has this author previously written or spoken on this topic or related topics?

5. Look at the table of contents or the list of entries or both.

   a. Is there a table of contents? Is it a strict listing of the contents in order? Is it in alphabetical order or arranged by subjects? Are there chapters or sections or just entries in alphabetical order?

   b. How are you going to access these materials? How might patrons access these materials?

   c. Peruse the list of entries or chapter headings. What do they tell you about the contents of the work? Are there any that appear to be missing or out of place?

6. Read some sample sections.

   a. Choose a section that you know a lot about, such as a science fiction chapter if you are a science fiction fan. How well does the information match what you know?

   b. Then choose another section that you know very little about. How informative is the entry or chapter? Does it make sense? Is enough background information provided?

7. Evaluate what you read. Will the average library patron be able to read and understand and use this work? Or is it best for librarians or serious fans? Is it accessible for teens or best for adults?

8. Who is the audience for this work? Is it aimed directly at readers, like Nancy Pearl's *Book Crush*? Or aimed at librarians working with readers, like Neil Hollands's *Read on . . . Fantasy Fiction*? Or is it best for librarians trying to understand the genre, like Saricks's *Readers' Advisory Guide to Genre Fiction* (2nd ed., 2009)?

9. How easy will this tool be to use at the desk with readers? Does it have annotations? Or will you need to look somewhere else for more information on every suggested author and title?

10. Consider the physical elements.

    a. Does the book open easily? Will it hold together as librarians use it?

    b. Is it too big or too small to fit easily on the reference shelves?

    c. If the book is going to circulate, will it hold up to multiple uses?

11. Check access points. How many ways are there to locate information?

    a. Author, subject, title, setting, and other indexes?

    b. Are there cross-references within the text? For example, under an entry for Nora Roberts, how are users guided to J. D. Robb, one of her pseudonyms?

    c. How useful is the table of contents?

    d. Are titles listed in more than one place?

    e. How easily can specific titles be located?

    f. How easily can read-alikes or reading suggestions be located?

12. If there is a previous edition, how similar or different is the new edition? Has the material been thoroughly updated? Are there significant changes?

ELECTRONIC SUBSCRIPTION SOURCES

The costs for subscription resources are generally much higher than for a single print source, and there are fewer to choose from, which just makes the initial evaluation that much more important. The good news is that anyone interested in purchasing can almost always get a free trial for detailed evaluation.

In addition to all the licensing issues a library must deal with in any electronic purchase, here are some special considerations for readers' advisors.

1. Go to the opening screen: what do you see?

   a. Can you find the search box?

   b. Is it obvious what should be typed into the search box? What is the default search? Is it a keyword search or a subject search or an author search? Can you tell if you need to type in the author's name or a subject heading in a certain way?

2. Check the Help and About Us sections: read these to learn more about the product.

   a. What is this resource about? Subject areas, coverage, and so on should all be dealt with here.

   b. What or who is this product designed for? Was it created with a specific reader or purpose in mind, or was it designed as a more general reference tool? Think about the differences between a general database like EBSCO's Academic Search and a very specific subject database like Library and Information Science Abstracts.

    c. How is this source supposed to be used? What kind of questions or problems was it designed to answer? Take the time to read about the advanced search features, limits, and controlled vocabulary.

3. Try a search. Choose something based on a real-life query from the desk or something that you know is popular, like Harry Potter read-alikes.

    a. Does your initial search strategy work?

       i. If so, what do you think of the results?

      ii. If not, are suggestions given for a better strategy?

4. Evaluate the search results: what comes up in the results list?

    a. How is the list formatted? Is it easy to read and/or understand? If it is a nontraditional display (like a visual map), how easy is it to understand? Would patrons like using it?

    b. What information is displayed? Is it helpful?

    c. If you click on the displayed links, what do you see?

    d. Are these results what you were expecting? Is anything missing? Is there anything that you weren't expecting but are pleased to see?

5. Consider the whole product.

    a. How easy is it to use? Will patrons be able to use it from home, or will they need help from librarians? Will all library staff be able to easily learn it and incorporate it into their daily work?

    b. What kinds of readers would find this resource most useful?

    c. What kinds of questions or reader problems is this tool going to answer?

    d. What other information or resources does it contain that might be helpful for professional development or passive readers' advisory (displays, lists, bookmarks, continuing education, feature articles, genre information, etc.)?

    e. Is it worth the price for library staff and readers?

6. Test it out. The best way to learn more about an electronic source is to use a real-life situation, such as a college-age adult who has just read the *Twilight* books and wants more like them.

    a. Try this query on a source (print or electronic) you're used to using and note the results.

    b. Try the same query on the new source.

       i. How easy was it to get an answer to your query?

      ii. Were you satisfied with the answer?

      iii. How does the new source compare to the known source?

    c. Try this test a few more times with different queries.

WEB-BASED RESOURCES

Web-based sources can be evaluated in nearly the same way as subscription sources. Here, however, the major concern is not whether the product fits into the budget but whether the library wants to recommend it as a good source for readers. In selecting web-based resources, the audience and the purpose for the selection are the most important factors. Is the resource a targeted list, like sites for mystery lovers? Or is it a more general guide to online RA sites? Will the list be mostly used by staff or by patrons visiting the library website? After answering these questions, use the same criteria and steps listed in the preceding section to evaluate any web-based tool.

WRITING THE REVIEW

After working through the preceding steps and considering all the key issues, compile your notes and start writing the review. Reference reviews are typically 350 to 400 words to allow plenty of space to address all the issues. If instead of a published review, you are writing an annotation or review for a library website, keep in mind your intended audience (probably the public) and try to avoid librarian jargon. When writing your review, make sure to answer these questions:

- What is the source about? What is the subject area and coverage?
- Who is the audience?
- How easy is it to use and access this source? Which and how many access points does it have? What about cross-references or hyperlinks? Do they work?
- What is the best section? The worst section?
- What are this resource's strengths and weaknesses?
- What kinds of questions or patron problems will it be able to answer?
- Is this source recommended?

Part 3

Marketing, Promoting, and
Sharing Materials

10

PASSIVE READERS' ADVISORY
Bookmarks, Booklists, and Displays

Lissa Staley

Bookmarks, themed booklists, and displays are not new concepts. Chances are high that you are already using these techniques in your library to promote collections and services. You also probably have an established routine for the way that you make a bookmark, set up a display, or create a booklist. Because you may already be doing many of the things mentioned in this chapter, I will focus on why librarians create booklists and displays and on ideas to help reinvigorate your creativity and inspire new publications and displays.

You do not have enough time to talk to each patron about her or his reading preferences and help find the perfect book, and some patrons may not appreciate this offer anyway. By creating timely and interesting displays, printed lists, and online lists, you can market library resources to your patrons and help them discover new titles on their own. Passive readers' advisory is an essential part of any library's readers' advisory services because it reaches a group of readers who cannot or will not take advantage of real-time or face-to-face services.

CHOOSING MATERIALS TO PROMOTE

You can promote absolutely anything using a bookmark, themed booklist, or display. We generally focus on promoting library materials that can be checked out, like books, audiobooks, movies, and music. Don't forget to promote children's materials, large print materials, and other special areas in your library's collection. Displays are a way to promote books that are hidden back in the stacks and bring them new readership. On booklists, consider including online resources, reference books, and any nonprofit community resources that support your theme.

To populate a display or booklist, gather materials of interest that customers would not likely discover on their own. The thought put into the title selections provides the underlying value of the booklist. Unless your booklist is specifically targeted to helping people place requests for items that have long waiting lists, concentrate on materials that are likely to be available for checkout soon. Unless you are promoting the advantages of interlibrary loan, make sure that your library owns all the materials you are promoting on your booklist. To find related materials on your topic, use all your readers' advisory resources, including subject-heading searching, online book reviews, booksellers' recommendations, other libraries' websites, the Fiction_L electronic discussion list, and your colleagues.

GETTING THREE FOR THE PRICE OF ONE

It is no coincidence that bookmarks, themed booklists, and displays are grouped together in a single chapter. These three items can frequently be produced at the same time using the same effort of brainstorming, research, and creativity to reach a variety of patrons over a period of time. While one reader browses the display in the library and checks out a few titles, another reader finds the bookmark and chooses titles to request, and a third reader accesses the themed booklist online while browsing the library website or searching the Internet. A one-week display can be used as a bookmark for a year and an online booklist indefinitely. When the display is repeated in the future, the bookmark and booklist can be updated with new titles.

CREATING AND DISPLAYING BOOKMARKS

The goal of a bookmark is to provide a visually appealing and convenient list for the patron. Bookmarks may either promote materials that are not being checked out, draw attention to related materials, or help people place requests on items that are checked out. Bookmarks also advertise programs and services.

Format bookmarks according to your library's publicity guidelines, which typically include a library logo, contact information, and library hours. Consider adding a statement of encouragement on how to find the materials listed, such as "Check availability of these titles using the online catalog at catalog.tscpl.org" or "If you need help locating these titles at the library, ask at the Reference Desk."

Choose a format that will be most helpful to the reader. If your fiction is arranged by author's last name, try a fiction bookmark that lists the author names prominently and is arranged alphabetically by author last name. Other arrangements that may fit particular situations include by title, by genre, in Dewey number order, by format, by publication date, or by topic.

Simple bookmarks can be created in a word-processing program and photocopied onto colored paper. Use cover art from book jackets to add visual appeal. Adding color printing, using graphic design software, or sending the job to a professional printer may increase the visual appeal of the bookmark. The more complicated the production process, the greater the expense and the delay between great idea and finished product. For large quantities of bookmarks, the in-house photocopier is usually less economical than outsourcing to a local printing business. If you are creating many bookmarks, pricing printing options and quantities may save money for your organization.

Every library displays bookmarks differently—in holders or racks, on bulletin boards or slat walls, on tables and counters, or even stuck in related books on the shelf. Don't limit your marketing of library materials only to current patrons in the building. Distribute health booklists in the waiting rooms of a local doctor's office, take parenting resource lists to day-care centers, and bring bookmarks promoting your print and online car repair manuals to the auto parts stores. Printed bookmarks are convenient for people to pick up and take with them. Because many of your patrons are accessing your library catalog remotely, provide bookmarks that can be accessed remotely as well. Several software options make it possible to save files as PDFs, which allow you to share your bookmarks on your website in an attractive printable format.

Online lists should take advantage of the medium—lists can link to other online resources and link titles to your library catalog. Because the advantages of online are sometimes the disadvantages of print, make sure your web page list prints nicely, and always try to offer a formatted and downloadable PDF of the list.

DEVELOPING THEMED BOOKLISTS

What is the difference between a bookmark and a themed booklist? Both items promote library materials by presenting recommended titles, but in this case, size matters. By definition, a bookmark should be small enough to mark one's place between the pages of a book. A booklist, on the other hand, is generally printed on standard letter-sized paper and may take the form of a small folded pamphlet, a stapled multipage handout, or anything in between. The creation, formatting, and display of booklists are similar to those of bookmarks. With the expanded format, booklists will generally contain more titles than a bookmark. Add brief annotations whenever space allows; the extra description will convey details and appeal factors to engage readers and help them in selecting titles.

DISPLAYING NEW MATERIALS

Chances are that your patrons like to see what is new at the library. Your new book and new movie sections are heavily browsed areas, and the circulation for those collections is higher than that for the corresponding areas in the stacks. Whether your library acknowledges this or not, if you have separate sections for new materials, you are already organizing and displaying these popular materials to better market them to your patrons.

The library uses a different stocking model than a bookstore, which receives weekly replenishment copies of any titles that are selling well. At the library, the most sought-after materials are checked out and have a waiting list, which leaves little incentive for people to come into the library to browse for popular titles. Some libraries designate a percentage of the copies of new best-selling titles to an "express" collection to increase browsing and reward readers who frequent the library building or bookmobiles. These express items may have a shorter checkout period and are not used to fill requests on the waiting list. Other libraries use rental collections to meet this need, and the entire rental collection becomes a default display of popular new materials.

DISPLAYING OLDER LIBRARY MATERIALS

Displays should draw attention to materials that patrons can check out. Any library will find it difficult to have a long-term display of the newest, hottest stuff. The goal of a display, unless it is under a glass case, is to connect patrons with books that they can borrow. Constantly refreshing and straightening and adding more materials is hard work, but it also signifies the success of your display and the dedication of the library to promoting reading.

Displays should not make it harder to find the materials because they are not on the shelves. Use location codes in the online catalog to reflect the display status of materials. If your library has multiple display areas, you can use several different display codes to direct patrons and staff to the correct locations.

Whether your library already has a weekly schedule for a shared display space or you are introducing displays for the first time, you can find inspiration from the following suggestions and examples.

GETTING CREATIVE

Try some small displays within the stacks. If you have money to make changes, use slanted display shelving, or you can simply shift books to create an empty shelf in the middle of a long range of books. Turn books face out to draw attention to popular authors or sections and add a related bookmark or booklist.

Adding displays to shelving end caps can promote collections and draw patrons into the stacks. If your budget allows, have end caps constructed to fit your shelves. Less expensive options are available for most standard-sized shelving units, such as a slat board backing with pegs for attaching book holders. On a smaller budget, use a spare table or barstool to add a tiny display area next to your stacks.

Use a special item to draw attention to the topic of your display: a cup and saucer for tea, knitting needles for crafts, a houseplant for gardening, a mixing bowl and whisk for cooking. Invite a community partner to make a display of items in a display case and provide related library materials and a themed booklist. Provide copies of the booklist for the community partner to distribute through its organization.

Programs promote collections, and themed lists can help promote the collection as well. An astronomy exhibit, a knitting workshop, a talk by a master gardener, or a lecture from a consumer health professional are all opportunities to create booklists and displays. Avoid including date-specific information on your booklist and you can continue to distribute it in the library for months afterward.

Put a display in an unexpected location. Display materials in another department, or add a display near a busy walkway in your library. A display that causes congestion in a hallway is bad, but a display that draws people toward an unused corner and helps them find more material to check out is good. Displaying materials away from their regular location in the library can also help draw attention to less used collections.

Use bookmarks to promote online resources and databases. A bookmark advertising the library's print and online auto repair resources can be displayed with the manuals in the library and distributed to local car parts stores. Do not be afraid to promote books and movies and music and websites at the same time, even on the same bookmark or display. Many stores selling books are also marketing movies and music to their customers. Why should the library be any different?

Libraries traditionally use read-alike lists based on a popular title or author. A traditional series list can be expanded to promote similar titles and authors that fans might enjoy. Consider basing a read-alike list on a movie or a television show like *CSI*, a national event like the presidential election, or an international event like the Olympics or World Cup. Using a news headline, like unrest in the Middle East, you can find related fiction and nonfiction to interest your patrons. Use and misuse of new technology can include both science fiction and nonfiction. More information on how to create read-alike lists can be found in chapter 12 of this book.

Bookmarks and booklists can bring together materials from across several cataloging areas. A booklist on a gluten-free diet may recommend titles from the sections for digestive diseases, specialty cookbooks, and personal stories of people diagnosed with celiac disease. Someone interested in one of those items is likely interested in the others, and a booklist can help connect the patron to the materials, even if the books do not sit together on the library shelves.

Bookmarks don't have to promote books. A list of great recipe websites can be useful to the patron browsing the cookbooks. Create a niche website list on a hobby or topic and distribute the bookmark in related books to advertise the availability of public computers or training classes as well as to connect customers to online resources.

Try these ideas to spice up your displays:

Experiment with displays that pair two types of materials: classic literature and classics retold, books and their film adaptations, Hollywood biographies and films starring the actors.

For audiobooks, try an "in their own words" display with audiobooks narrated by their authors.

A "lost in the stacks" display can feature books that have not been checked out in the past few years.

Draw attention to micro-histories like *Salt* and *Cod*.

Try displaying Danielle Steel novels backward, with many years of author photos showing.

For a fun and easy visual display, choose materials based on the cover art of the book. Walk through the fiction stacks pulling all the pink books or all the black-and-red covers. For a more ambitious display, search out covers with images of dogs, shoes, or half-naked men.

A display on ecotourism can bring together earth-friendly armchair travel items, including books about safaris, bird-watching guides, DVD documentaries like *Planet Earth* and travel films, coffee-table photography books featuring national parks and underwater photography, and travel guidebooks about state parks. Put up a sign promoting related magazines such as *Canoe and Kayak, Outside, National Parks, National Geographic Adventure,* and *Birder's World,* and remind patrons that checking out library books about their dream destinations saves them money and resources.

A "sense of place" display can feature a mix of fiction and nonfiction books set in Florida or books that capture the essence of Florida and various places in the state, including mystery novels, travelogues, and photography books.

When you visit other libraries while on vacation (don't we all do this?) check out the bookmarks and booklists displayed there for additional inspiration. Throughout your career, you will encounter more great display, bookmark, and themed booklist ideas, probably more than you will ever actually use. Jot down the ideas that appeal to you and try to offer them at your library as you have time and motivation.

SHARING IDEAS

At Pamunkey Regional Library (Virginia), each staff member participated in creating a series of bookmarks to share with other regional librarians and patrons, and the library published over two hundred examples online.[1]

Iowa Library Service Areas provides bookmarks for other libraries in Word format for downloading. You can customize these resources to your library and your collection.[2]

Multnomah County (Oregon) Library offers adult and teen booklists by category, with online booklists linked to the library catalog.[3]

Pierce County (Washington) Library System creates topical, annotated online booklists for kids and teens. The lists are linked to the library catalog, and customers are encouraged to write a review of any title.[4]

Washington County (Oregon) Cooperative Library Services promotes its large print collections with downloadable PDF booklists designed in a large print layout to better serve readers.[5]

NOTES

1. Pamunkey Regional Library (Virginia), "Staff Bookmark Slide Shows," www .pamunkeylibrary.org/bookmark_slides.htm.

2. Iowa Library Service Areas, "Readers' Advisory: If you like . . . Bookmarks," www.ilsa.lib.ia.us/readadvice.htm#bookmarks.

3. Multnomah County (Oregon) Library, "Adult and Teen Booklists by Category," www.multcolib.org/books/lists/adultlists.html.

4. Pierce County (Washington) Library System, "Booklists for Teens," www .piercecountylibrary.org/kids-teens/teens/book-lists-teens/Default.htm.

5. Washington County (Oregon) Cooperative Library Services, "What to Read?" www.wccls.org/library_services/homebound/what_to_read.html.

11

CREATING THEMED BOOKLISTS

Lynne Welch

Librarians put a great deal of time, effort, and money into continually updating their collections, and they naturally wish to maximize their investments by ensuring that readers can find the books that are most appropriate at any given time. Themed booklists are an important tool for readers' advisory, and one that can be part of any library's services. Librarians use themed booklists in many ways. They may serve as a handy reference for readers' advisory staff working with the public. They may also be used passively in readers' advisory; staff need not conduct readers' advisory interviews in order for readers to find the books they would like to read. Themed booklists should always be part of displays that address specific topics and draw attention to the library's holdings. Readers appreciate being able to pick up a list of suggested books to carry with them to the shelves or to look for later. Another use for booklists is to create buzz, or interest, in otherwise neglected areas of the collection. Last, booklists can be a great way to enhance the RA presence on your library website and reach out to readers who don't visit the physical desk. Creating topical or "themed" booklists, therefore, becomes a useful skill for the readers' advisor.

TYPES OF BOOKLISTS AND COMMON CHARACTERISTICS

Themed booklists are built around shared elements. These may include

- genre (books of a particular literary type, such as poetry or chick lit)
- character types (such as the caterer-turned-amateur-detective)
- setting (including both place and time period)

- subject (this can refer to an actual controlled-vocabulary subject heading in the library catalog or to a topic or style of writing, such as "black Christian fiction")
- author (by region, by ethnicity, or in comparison with another author; read-alikes, discussed in chapter 12 of this book, are a specialized form of booklist)
- audience (books aimed at or appealing to a particular group, such as teen boys, senior citizens, or book club members)
- quality (the annual "best of" lists produced by magazines, reader groups, and professional organizations)
- miscellaneous (mostly compiled for marketing purposes, such as "Books with Red Covers" or "Here Today, Gone Tomorrow unless you check them out")

Booklists may be composed entirely of fiction, nonfiction, or a mixture of the two, depending on the intended purpose. Booklists may also include video, music, and periodical resources. And don't forget the information to be found in any online databases to which the library subscribes! Although these lists are called *book*lists there is no reason not to expand into other areas of the collection as appropriate. Integrated Advisory, which uses all types of materials found in a library collection, is especially effective in larger libraries where people may not be aware of all the resources offered by the library, or even in smaller libraries that struggle to keep book-only displays full.

"Mysteries set in Montana" might be the theme of one such list; "Our canine companions" could be another. Nonfiction titles are easily compiled by searching the library catalog using both keywords and controlled vocabulary, but it may take more digging to come up with fiction titles, because many libraries do not fully catalog their fiction holdings.

SOURCES FOR BOOKLIST ITEMS

The topic for a booklist is often dictated by need. Someone visits or calls the library, and the staff discovers that they have no ready suggestions in answer to a reader query. If you find it difficult to build a booklist around a particular theme, consider posting a request for title recommendations to the Fiction_L electronic discussion list.[1] By the way, this site does not limit itself to discussions about works of fiction! Nonfiction topics, and indeed all readers' advisory issues, are also appropriate subjects for the group. Another option is to consult one of the online booksellers such as Amazon.com, Borders, or Barnes and Noble; a keyword search will yield many suggestions. A third is to make use of the many excellent commercial readers' advisory databases and resources. Some of these, like Gale's Literature Resource Center, EBSCOhost's NoveList, and the Reader's Advisor Online from Libraries Unlimited, are available electronically. Others, including works from ALA, Libraries Unlimited, and Thomson Gale, utilize a print format. Of course, you should independently evaluate each title thus gleaned for suitability in your particular circumstances, but all of these resources do provide a useful starting point for titles you might not otherwise consider.

The Morton Grove (Illinois) Public Library, which hosts the Fiction_L mailing list, has compiled a huge collection of Fiction_L's booklists and has made them freely available to the public.[2] Various search options are provided for ease of use. They include keyword searching and an option to search by date.

Another useful online service is provided by Fantastic Fiction, a privately maintained British website offering author photos and biographical information, website links, and cover art where available.[3] The site also groups titles in series and includes authors and works in some of the emerging subgenres not covered elsewhere.

PURPOSES OF THEMED BOOKLISTS

In addition to stimulating interest in particular titles or authors, booklists can aid in marketing the collection as a whole. For example, January is the month when many people decide to diet and exercise. A themed booklist can pull together the how-to books as well as entertaining true first-person accounts of people trying to lose weight and fictional stories about characters who do so and what happens next in their lives. You may also wish to spotlight instructional videos on various ways to exercise (including dancing and yoga), cookbooks, any foodie magazines to which the library subscribes, music CDs to get people up and moving, and so on. Encourage readers to select any items that catch their interest by posting relevant booklists near the highlighted collections.

Another purpose for themed booklists is to support school curricula. Whether or not your library's stated mission is to support your local schools, you will probably encounter students and parents who need help with assignments. When you realize that numerous students are seeking information on the same topic, or you are fortunate enough to be alerted by the school that a topic will be in great demand, you can assemble a booklist for use by staff and students. This is especially helpful when the topic is not a familiar one or will require extensive and detailed knowledge of the collection as a whole, rather than of just one section.

Imagine a week in which some high school students are seeking information on the French resistance efforts during World War II, while others are researching the causes and effects of Manifest Destiny, and every fourth-grader in town needs to write a report on exotic and endangered animals. Assigning staff members to become familiar with specific topics and to compile themed booklists will pay off in the long run, especially for frontline staff who may otherwise be surprised when a student or parent approaches with a request for information on a topic with which staff are unfamiliar.

Yet another way to promote your collection is to find an unusual thread to draw together neglected and overlooked items in the collection. "Books with red covers" or "Books from the bottom shelf" or "Last chance (books to be weeded)" are all fun yet intriguing themes that may draw attention to items that might otherwise be discarded due to lack of circulation.

One caveat: if you are writing a booklist for any of the preceding reasons, please limit it to items actually owned by your library! (You may also choose to list items readily available through the local consortia.) There is nothing more frustrating to a reader than to find a nice long list of items that sound perfectly suited to his or her need, only to discover that the library doesn't have any of them. Readers will understand if someone else is currently using a title, but they will become very unhappy with a list that showcases intriguing titles not in your collection.

Sometimes booklists are compiled to provide readers with a definitive list of titles by an author, including their series name and order where applicable. The Kent District Library (KDL) in Michigan offers a very useful online resource for people trying to track down the various books in a series, appropriately called What's Next.[4] Print versions are also available directly from KDL; ordering information is at the bottom of the What's Next online search page.

ORGANIZATION AND PRESENTATION OF BOOKLISTS

Generally, booklist titles are organized in some basic fashion—by date of publication, or alphabetically by title or author. A short annotation for each title is always helpful (see chapter 6 in this book on creating annotations and reviews), as is the call number of each item so people know where to find it. A booklist may be lengthy or very limited in scope, depending on the subject matter and the number of available resources. A good rule of thumb is to provide at least eight to ten titles, with brief annotations. Give your booklist a catchy title based on its theme (the genre, characters, setting, etc.), and you need not repeat that information in each annotation. The bookmark format (either three or four columns, printed in landscape format on a letter-sized page [8½ by 11 inches]) is very useful as a take-along for members of the public, as they can carry it with them, and is quite economical to produce in quantity. The booklist need not be printed on cardstock or with colored inks; regular copier paper in an eye-catching hue, printed in black, is quite adequate. You may also choose to create the booklist on only one side (in which case the reader may use the reverse to take notes) or both (if you have plenty of titles to fill both sides).

Some libraries, instead of printing quantities of individual booklists for each member of the reading public to take, prefer to assemble their booklists in a "book of good books." This is often kept at a staff member's desk, but it may be placed in a publicly accessible area instead. A three-ring binder, with letter-sized pages (8½ by 11 inches) printed on front and back and encased in protective plastic, is very useful, as the individual lists may be removed from the binder as needed and taken to the shelves. This format is also much easier to maintain, as library staff can see at a glance what topics may require an update and copies need not be perpetually replenished.

WRITING A BOOKLIST

The first order of business should be to decide upon your subject, its parameters and limitations. Sometimes the subject is limited by a lack of titles; at other times, it is sufficiently broad to require you to limit your scope. For example, at one point there was a profusion of cozy mystery series featuring cats, and each series offered multiple titles. In this case, it might be easiest to provide one list containing "authors of cozy mysteries featuring cats" and to provide the author name, series name, and initial title within the series, together with a brief annotation about the series as a whole. Main character (including feline) names and the perceived appeal of this particular series (Does the cat solve the mysteries? Does the cat have peculiarly endearing characteristics? Does the cat talk?) should be described as succinctly as possible. Then another list could be created for each such author, listing all the titles in series order, with a brief annotation for each title; or directions for accessing What's Next or NoveList could be added to the bookmark as a way to encourage readers to try out the library's RA tools. This sounds like a lot of work, but the fifteenth time in one week you are asked for the new Lilian Jackson Braun, or "someone who writes like her," you will be grateful you have that information readily available! Also, remember that the copy/paste function of your word-processing program can be put to good use. Why type every list manually when you can go online and grab the information, paste it into a new document using the "paste special—unformatted text" function, and be done in a fraction of the time?

Next, consider all the ways this subject may be addressed. Include keyword terms (everyday language) as well as the controlled-vocabulary Library of Congress subject headings found in the library's catalog. Also take a moment to consider other aspects of your topic. For example, the "Manifest Destiny causes and effects" research project required first a working knowledge of the term itself. Consulting *World Book,* or another basic encyclopedia, allows the booklist compiler to focus on several aspects of this historical phenomenon: Lewis and Clark's early expeditions, the Louisiana Purchase, the U.S. annexation of Texas, the California Gold Rush of 1849, and the Oregon Trail are a few. List the items cataloged with those subject headings, but remember that the library catalog does not generally address what is *inside* the books, so you will also want to visit the shelves and check the table of contents and index of any other likely resources, keeping in mind the list of terms, persons, and events you have brainstormed. In this way, you will help hopeful researchers to incorporate all sorts of informational tidbits, thereby lending color and interest to their finished product.

Including online research strategies, especially with regard to particularly relevant commercial subscription databases of which your public may be unaware, is always helpful. To do this, cite the database name and how to access it, as well as your specific search strategy. For example:

To access the Academic Search Premier database,

- visit www.ohioweblibrary.org
- click on Resources
- click on Academic Search Premier
- type ["Manifest Destiny" causes]; the brackets indicate the search box

You should also be aware that some search engines may provide additional options in the form of audio, video, and image files as well as textual references. These can further enrich the research experience and enhance the finished product.

Decide how you want to format the booklist: will it be a bookmark with limited space for suggestions, or full-sized sheets? Also decide how you will organize the title suggestions: by format, perhaps, and by call number within each format. Or, in the case of a broad topic requiring information from several subject areas, such as Manifest Destiny, it may be more helpful to organize resources by subject area, so that researchers can proceed directly to the resources most pertinent to their chosen concentrations.

Always begin your booklist by identifying your organization, with at least its name and city/state. It is useful to provide contact information as well, perhaps at the bottom. Title the booklist: be clever, but make your subject clear. Some compilers of booklists add graphic-design elements, such as eye-catching fonts and small images, to attract attention. A booklist on fantasy, for example, may scatter dragons, wizard's wands, and more about the page. Be careful: do not become so enraptured by the artistic elements that they overwhelm the text!

Next, begin your list. Pulling the actual items from the shelves is often helpful, as you can use the cover, as well as the promotional blurbs on the jacket and back, for inspiration when writing the annotation. Visiting the shelves also allows you to become familiar with other topics that may tie in to your theme and to establish a mental frame of reference. You may also discover that some of the titles you selected, although showing available in the catalog, are actually missing from the collection. This is fortunate from the readers' standpoint because you will not include titles they have no hope of finding, but also from the library's standpoint, as it can serve as a prompt to update holdings information and to consider additional items for purchase.

Finally, create your list (various examples appear on the following pages). Remember that it can be printed as well as posted to your library website. Post a copy of the final product online in the PDF format; your public will thank you. Keep digital copies of perennially recurring topics, such as series booklists and subject reports assigned every year by the local schools, on file as well. That way, you can easily update and reprint/repost them as necessary, and your colleagues will also thank you!

Notes

1. Morton Grove (Illinois) Public Library, "Welcome to Fiction_L!" www.webrary .org/RS/FLmenu.html.
2. Morton Grove (Illinois) Public Library, "Fiction_L Archives," www.webrary .org/RS/FLarchive.html.
3. Fantastic Fiction, www.fantasticfiction.co.uk.
4. Kent District (Michigan) Public Library, "What's Next," ww2.kdl.org/libcat/ WhatsNextNEW.asp.

BEST FRIENDS FOREVER: OUR DOGS

by Lynne Welch

What is it about the combination of dogs and books that makes dog books so popular? From childhood icons such as Spot and Lassie to celebrity and presidential pets, we seem to have an insatiable appetite for reading about the enduring, deeply passionate connection we share with our furry friends. As Groucho Marx allegedly remarked, "Outside of a dog, a book is man's best friend. Inside of a dog, it's too dark to read." And readers, well supplied by the publishing industry, eagerly search out books on our canine companions and their relationships with their own particular humans.

John Steinbeck, the distinguished novelist and inveterate wanderer, set out on a road trip across America with a French poodle named Charley, chronicling their adventures in search of that indefinable quality which makes this country and its people unique. *Travels with Charley: In Search of America* is the result of that journey and for almost fifty years has been a beloved favorite of readers in the genre. Learned and erudite, Steinbeck is nonetheless a very accessible author, and his introspection can be quite amusing.

At roughly the same time and across the pond in England, James Herriot (real name: James Alfred "Alf" Wight) was transcribing his own adventures as a veterinary surgeon working and living in a sleepy little Yorkshire country village. *All Creatures Great and Small,* an omnibus edition comprising two of his first releases, and its successor volumes are familiar at least by name to most readers. They comprise a memoir of his personal as well as his professional life, through which Herriot set the standard for books about country life with companion animals. In the process, he introduced generations of readers to this type of anecdotal narrative, which continues to be extremely popular among all ages. *James Herriot's Dog Stories* and *James Herriot's Favorite Dog Stories* are collections of anecdotes focusing exclusively on the canine world.

Marley and Me: Life and Love with the World's Worst Dog hit and remained on the *New York Times* best-seller list for months because, more than a paean to doggyness itself or a specific specimen thereof, it celebrated the unique bond between human and canine, in spite of numerous failings and foibles on both sides. Author John Grogan, a journalist by profession, details his family's history with Marley in a matter-of-fact narrative encompassing all aspects of their life together. Spanning the whole range between sadness and hilarity, *Marley and Me* draws on the emotional connection humans form with their dogs.

Another such detailed commentary is the classic *My Dog Tulip,* by J. R. Ackerley, written over fifty years ago and still in print due to continued demand. Condemned by some readers for what they term its almost pathological obsession with the

(cont.)

animal's scatological functions, the book nonetheless offers intriguing insights into the passionate attachments some people form with their nonhuman companions.

From Baghdad, with Love: A Marine, the War, and a Dog Named Lava is the enthralling story of a group of Marines calling themselves the Lava Dogs and the tiny puppy they rescued, fed, raised, and finally brought to the United States to start a new life with the narrator, Lieutenant Colonel Jay Kopelman. A riveting and suspenseful story of survival as well as a grippingly poignant, no-holds-barred exposé detailing the reality of life for our military as well as the native population, both human and animal, in Iraq, Lava's story reminds us that so many times, it is the measure of our humanity to care for the helpless as individuals worthy of our attention and support, rather than as targets or opportunities for propaganda efforts.

Disaster takes only a moment to change life as we know it, and Abigail Thomas details how she coped, with the aid of her husband's pets, when he was left for dead by a hit-and-run driver while out jogging. Her memoir, *A Three Dog Life,* is a testament to her courage and resilience, her loyalty to her husband and his beloved dogs, and her determination to make the most of the limited relationship now possible with Rich, whose brain was traumatized and who thereafter was confined to a nursing facility that specialized in treating those types of injuries.

By contrast, many authors choose to write short, snappy works exhibiting humor and whimsy. Peter Mayle, author of the much-beloved *A Year in Provence,* penned a novel purporting to be the memoirs of his dog Boy and titled *A Dog's Life,* which has also been translated into audio format with great success.

Another who writes in this vein is Louise Bernikow, and her woman-meets-dog story is presented in two volumes: *Bark If You Love Me* introduces the author as a single woman living in the city, content with her solitary existence until a small brown boxer moves in and changes her life forever. The sequel, *Dreaming in Libro: How a Good Dog Tamed a Bad Woman,* continues their story until the animal is finally laid to rest, but not without forever changing the author. Writing in a frank, conversational style, Bernikow confesses to her transformation from an independent career woman to a dog person.

Pulitzer Prize winner Anna Quindlen reflects, briefly but charmingly, on the life of the family's beloved black Labrador, Beau, and how she is the richer for his companionship. *Good Dog. Stay.* is written with her signature insights and humor. This tribute to Beau's unending good humor, loyalty, and ability to live fully in the present is interspersed throughout with entertaining photographs of myriad breeds and personalities of dogs and would make a good introduction to anyone who doesn't understand the appeal of Man's Best Friend.

Jon Katz is another who has written volumes about the various animal denizens of his back-to-nature experiment, which he laughingly christens Bedlam Farm. *Dog Days: Dispatches from Bedlam Farm* is the latest in the series (preceded by *A Good Dog: The Story of Orson, Who Changed My Life; The Dogs of Bedlam Farm;* and *A Dog Year: Twelve Months, Four Dogs, and Me*). Offering somewhat of a compromise between the journalistic chronicles of Grogan and the self-deprecating brief narratives of Mayle and Bernikow, Katz, a city boy, tackles country life and his inevitable misadventures in a delightfully insouciant fashion.

Poignant, revealing, thought-provoking: *Merle's Door: Lessons from a Freethinking Dog* is, as its title implies, more than just another dog story. Author Ted Kerasote researched canine genealogy and the evolution of human-dog interactions for two years before distilling that knowledge into this humorously conversational account detailing his first meeting with Merle on a rafting trip, his realization of the dog's potential and subsequent decision to offer him a home, and his desire to facilitate Merle's continued growth and happiness. Flying in the face of conventional wisdom, he proceeded to treat Merle as an equal, and the results astounded casual observers and close friends alike.

Anthologies provide another avenue for learning about our fascination with and affinity for the nonhumans who cohabit our living spaces and invade our hearts. *The Wonderful Thing about Pets* by Gary Burghoff features a series of short, heartwarming vignettes exploring the remarkable animals including dogs who share and enrich the lives of various humans. Former actor Burghoff, a wildlife artist and owner of an animal rehab center in Malibu, California, hosted the public television show *Pets: Part of the Family.*

One subgenre of companion-animal literature is the celebrity companion animal—that animal who might be no more special than your dog or mine, were it not for the notoriety achieved by its owner. From Dolley Madison's parrot to Laura Bush's cats and dogs, Americans have a long history of interest in life as lived in the White House, especially by pets.

Dear Socks, Dear Buddy is former First Lady Hillary Rodham Clinton's contribution to the genre, providing a brief history of White House pets and featuring letters received by the Clintons' dog and cat from animal lovers of all ages. The photos enhance the anecdotal read, full of personalities and minutiae but expressing to a nicety the concerns of the American public regarding presidential animals.

Millie's Book was "dictated" to Barbara Bush and reveals the life of the First Dog on the campaign trail as well as during her tenure in the White House. Lighthearted and amusing, this book will appeal to readers who enjoyed the memoirs of Peter Mayle's dog as well as to those interested in the behind-the-scenes life of White House residents.

Whether profiling superstars or more ordinary folk, the celebration of life reflected in these accounts of life with our canine companions guarantees their continuing popularity among readers for the foreseeable future.

Lynne Welch is an Ohio librarian specializing in Readers' Advisory and Electronic Reference Services.

March 2008, NoveList and EBSCOhost

INTRODUCTION TO KNITTING: SOME USEFUL RESOURCES

Herrick Memorial Library
Wellington, Ohio

Books (please visit the Nonfiction section, number 746.43, for more titles)

First Knits: Projects for Beginning Knitters (Luise Roberts and Kate Haxell)

A to Z of Knitting: The Ultimate Guide for the Beginner to Advanced Knitter

One-Skein Wonders (edited by Judith Durant)

Getting Started Knitting Socks (Ann Budd)

Teach Yourself Visually: Knitting Design; Working from a Master Pattern to Fashion Your Own Knits (Sharon Turner)

Stephanie Pearl-McPhee Casts Off: The Yarn Harlot's Guide to the Land of Knitting

Magazines

Creative Knitting—just added to the library's collection

Videos by Lucy Neatby: A Knitter's Companion

Knitting Essentials 1 and *2*

Knitting Gems 3

Sock Techniques 1 and *2*

Stories by and about people who knit

Debbie Macomber's Blossom Street series (*The Shop on Blossom Street, Back on Blossom Street,* etc.)

Knit Together: Discover God's Pattern for Your Life, by Debbie Macomber

The Friday Night Knitting Club—a novel by Kate Jacobs

Some useful websites

http://techknitting.blogspot.com—knitting techniques explained

www.knittingpatterncentral.com—free patterns

www.knitpicks.com/Patterns/Knitting_Patterns.html—some free, some for purchase

www.youtube.com—for video tutorials of knitting skills

www.google.com—for diagrams, instructions, and video tutorials of knitting skills

http://knittingonthenet.com—more free patterns

www.interweaveknits.com—free patterns and the chance to sign up for a daily newsletter delivered to your e-mail

EXPLORE NEW WORLDS IN SCIENCE FICTION!

Diplomatic Immunity—Lois McMaster Bujold: Humorous space opera featuring the continuing adventures of Lord Miles Vorkosigan, that resourceful intergalactic Imperial Troubleshooter, on his honeymoon. Call no.: (FICTION) BUJ

Down and Out in the Magic Kingdom—Cory Doctorow: In this fast-moving short read, people live forever by cloning their bodies and transferring their memories, and Jules discovers a plot to take over the DisneyWorld rides. Call no.: (FICTION) DOC

Pattern Recognition—William Gibson: Cayce is a coolhunter; she sniffs out the next trends before they're popular and gets involved in a worldwide Internet-based cult and the Russian Mafia, among others. Call no.: (FICTION) GIB

Dune: The Battle of Corrin—Frank Herbert: The latest in the classic series about the rise and fall of empires caught up in galactic war between humans and computers on the desert planet called Dune. Call no.: (FICTION) HER

Souls in the Great Machine—Sean McMullen: In 40th-century Australia, technology is forbidden, but attacks from both sea and sky convince Zarzora that it is their only hope for survival. Call no.: (FICTION) MCM

New Voices in Science Fiction—edited by Mike Resnick: Twenty short stories by some of the most promising new authors writing today, including time-travel, vampires, new takes on fairy tales, and more. Call no.: (FICTION) NEW

Finders Keepers—Linnea Sinclair: Wisecracking bootleg freighter captain Trilby Elliott and arrogant, by-the-book Imperial military officer Rhis Vanur join forces to thwart the evil 'Sko who want to take over the galaxy in this rollicking space adventure. Call no.: (FICTION) SIN

Cryptonomicon—Neal Stephenson: A very dense, highly detailed read for those who enjoy math puzzles, secret codes, and treasure hunts. Two parallel stories, one set in World War II and the other happening now, and three families are intertwined in this epic adventure. Call no.: (FICTION) STE

Herrick Memorial Library
101 Willard Memorial Square
Wellington, OH
440-647-2120

12

READ-ALIKES

Lynne Welch

Readers' advisory is about making connections—between readers and the books they may enjoy, and between books offering a similar reading experience. But it's also about making distinctions. A skilled readers' advisor learns to evaluate and articulate the underlying reasons why some books in widely divergent genres appeal to a particular reader, while other books in the same genre or covering the same subject matter may not. When performing readers' advisory, it is important to remember that the objective is different from the one-time reference interview in that you are engaging readers in a continuing conversation and that there are no correct answers, merely options. By adopting the habit of suggesting a range of titles the reader may wish to explore, rather than recommending any specific titles based on personal experience, you place yourself on an equal level with the reader, rather than appearing to be a judge of his or her tastes. This method encourages a more honest exchange, and over time can result in a rewarding interchange of opinions, as your readers gradually become more comfortable approaching you.

A read-alike is one of the tools used in readers' advisory. It is a special kind of booklist, with specific criteria and guidelines, but basically it is an annotated booklist (see chapter 6, "Reviews and Annotations for Fiction and Nonfiction," and chapter 11, "Creating Themed Booklists," for more information on these topics). Booklists generally explore one shared element: subject matter, setting, or genre, for example. By contrast, the read-alike addresses all aspects of an author's personal writing style, or the many ways in which a particular title appeals to a certain segment of the reading population. The read-alike then suggests other authors and books that may provide a similar combination of appeals.

THE ELEMENTS OF WRITING

Each time you create a useful read-alike, you sharpen your skills as a readers' advisor by learning more about that subset of literature. A careful examination of your subject also increases your awareness and understanding of the nuances of writing which, when combined, create a particular reading experience. These elements of writing include

- story
- characters
- language
- mood
- setting
- author voice

Story includes themes as well as the central action and any subplots the author has chosen to incorporate. *Characters* can be broadly interpreted as persons or other sentient beings as well as any other elements—such as a forbidding landscape—playing a part in the setup and resolution of the story. *Language* refers to the amount of description versus dialogue and the complexity of words as well as to the way in which they are used. For example, short sentences, especially when combined with a great deal of dialogue, allow the reader to progress more quickly through the pages and thus will make a book seem more fast-paced than will lengthy descriptive passages. *Mood* describes the atmosphere or emotions evoked by the author, while *setting* includes both time and place. *Author voice* is an elusive quality best summed up as "writing style," or the way the author uses all these elements. In the process, he or she often builds brand-name recognition, and fans of a particular writing style learn to recognize it even when the author is not identified. Conversely, some authors choose to make their voice transparent, bland almost, so that story, rather than style, is the focus. Nora Roberts is one such author.

Joyce Saricks, in *Readers' Advisory Service in the Public Library*, cites four "appeal elements," which look at these six aspects of writing from a slightly different perspective.[1] Saricks examines these elements:

- pacing (how language and author voice combine to enhance the reader's sense of internal tension and external conflict)
- characterization
- story line
- frame (the physical and temporal setting, as well as the atmosphere or mood fostered in the reader)

Both approaches are valid; the trick is to find the one that works better for you and to practice until you are comfortable using it.

The Readers' Advisory Guide to Genre Fiction, also by Saricks, explores the appeal elements of various types of genre fiction and provides benchmark authors for each.[2] Another resource with which you should become familiar is the Chicago-area Adult Reading Round Table, which conducts yearly in-depth genre studies and posts its conclusions, along with helpful vocabulary for the use of any interested readers' advisor, to the organization's website.[3] The Williamsburg (Virginia) Regional Library (WRL) offers an online questionnaire designed to get the reader thinking about the traits he or she prizes in books.[4] The WRL questionnaire is also valuable to the readers' advisor as a source of descriptive vocabulary and as a reminder of the many factors working together to create a satisfactory experience for the reader.

FOCUSING THE READ-ALIKE

On occasion, a read-alike will focus on the particular reading experience provided by a single title. This can be because the book is radically different from the rest of an author's output, or it may simply indicate immense popularity and, therefore, recurrent demands for "more just like this." Dan Brown's *Da Vinci Code* offers one such memorable example. Brown had written several novels before this one achieved such prominence in the minds of readers and nonreaders alike that everyone, whether a reader or not, wanted to read it. It behooves the readers' advisor to keep abreast of such trends, in order to be prepared with alternate suggestions when yet another reader requests a popular title with a lengthy hold list.

More often, a read-alike discusses the body of an author's work in general, citing the nature of each appeal element, mentioning any exceptions, and offering a suggested starting point for readers new to this author. Then the read-alike may list a number of authors and titles that provide a similar reading experience and provide brief annotations for each. This is the model used by the NoveList database as well as by many of the print resources such as *Genreflecting.* This model has proved to be popular with readers and librarians alike because it spells out author appeal, with specific examples of the ways in which suggested titles provide a good match.

When creating a read-alike for narrative nonfiction, the subject matter is an obvious focus, but not all readers approach reading in the same way or for the same reasons. Some readers enjoy thoroughly investigating a particular subject area and will read anything written on the topic. Other readers might choose a particular title because they have read other books by this author and discovered a preference for the writing style. Readers might also consider the author's attention to historical detail, the author's approach to the subject matter (perhaps he uses a relatively minor historical figure's perspective or that of the underdog rather than the victor), and whether additional supplementary materials (e.g., maps, primary sources, and photos or illustrations) are present. Tone is important, too; fans of true crime or wartime histories relish graphic descriptions; others might prefer a more sanitized version.

Each story—whether fiction or nonfiction—creates a particular atmosphere for the reader, and the objectives in creating a read-alike are to pinpoint the elements that create that atmosphere and to brainstorm other titles, whether or not they cover the same subject, that offer a similar reading experience. This is why it is so important to include annotations and to explicitly describe the particular factors making each author or title or both a good match in your own read-alikes.

WRITING A READ-ALIKE: THE CHALLENGES

Not all readers' advisors work in large, well-stocked libraries, and it can be challenging to construct useful read-alikes even with that advantage. For the library staff member who is not permitted time off the desk to become familiar with new releases and to work undisturbed, the writing task is even more challenging.

Getting Started

Ideally, you should first provide yourself with the selected author's biography and bibliography as well as all of her or his books. By reading a large number of an author's titles in a relatively limited time span, you will begin to notice recurring elements. Perhaps the author has a trick with dialogue or a way with description that is noteworthy. Some authors tell the same story over and over, with different character and place names. Others tell a new story each time and amaze their readers by the creativity and imagination they bring to each new release. Some writers concentrate exclusively on a particular period in history or always write on a nonfiction subject in a particular field.

If complete immersion in your assigned topic is not practical, you should at least try to physically handle the items, using the skills presented in chapter 1, "How to Read a Book in Ten Minutes." With practice, this technique will allow you to gain some idea of the author's style. Another source of information is the evaluative review, from resources such as *Booklist* or *Library Journal*. These brief critical examinations offer valuable information about a book from an impartial perspective, and the really useful ones also offer insights into the author's chosen themes, as well as a discussion of the title compared to the author's previous body of work.

For those titles you are unable to read in full, you may wish to consult one of the online booksellers and read not only the plot synopses provided as "editorial reviews" by the publisher but also the critical reviews and the reviews by the public. Other useful resources include the following:

- The author's web page, which may offer excerpts for evaluating the author's style (your preferred search engine should be able to provide the URL, especially if you formulate your search string using quotation marks around the first and last name of the author to indicate a phrase, for example ["Dan Brown" official website], where the brackets indicate the search box)

- Online review sources such as blogs and professional organizations supporting the genre

- Fantastic Fiction, a British site offering links to author web pages, brief biographies, and cover art in addition to series listings[5]

- What's Next, a free online searchable database of sequels maintained by the Kent District Library (Michigan)[6]

- Commercial databases such as NoveList, the Gale Literature Resource Center, and The Reader's Advisor Online

Filling In the Gaps

Once you have gained an understanding of your primary author, you should brainstorm other authors whose titles evoke a similar feeling in the reader. Perhaps you have access to specific readers' advisory resources, either print or electronic, that will provide other recommendations. Evaluative book reviews will come in handy once more, as the more helpful ones will include comparisons to other authors in the genre.

Do not forget your colleagues, both within the library and in Library-land generally! Frontline staff, especially, are an often overlooked, but knowledgeable, source of information. They see what circulates on a regular basis and can frequently discern patterns and provide insight into the titles and genres your readers enjoy. Especially if you have been assigned to construct a read-alike on a topic or author with which you may be relatively unfamiliar, it makes sense to ask for recommendations from anyone who prefers to read on that topic or in that genre. The successful readers' advisor will compile a list of friends, family, and acquaintances—perhaps the staff at other libraries or at a local bookstore—who read in various areas and will share their expertise upon request. A sample table, aptly titled "Who Reads What," is appended at the end of this chapter. You may wish to use it as a staff development "getting to know you" exercise, with prizes for the most successful participant. Or you can just fill in the table for your personal or department's reference. Do consider customizing the table with the categories you often encounter and in a way that makes sense to you.

Another source of suggestions is the Internet. Since 2007, the Collection Development and Evaluation Section (CODES) of the Reference and User Services Association (RUSA), a division of ALA, compiles The Reading List of exceptional genre fiction in various categories, with suggestions of other titles in each genre.[7] And Phil Eskew, who teaches the Readers' Advisory for Adults course in the School of Library and Information Science at Indiana University, has posted a number of sample bookmarks and read-alikes created by his students on subjects of their choice.[8] Many other places, including public libraries and the Fiction_L discussion list, have compiled extensive booklists and shared them freely online. Unfortunately, some of these latter lists are not annotated, which reduces their usefulness, but an Internet search using either [if you like "Author Name"] or [authors like "Dean Koontz"] should yield at least some helpful pointers. Please remember to research each title to ensure it satisfies your own criteria, but the author and title suggestions these lists produce can provide an invaluable starting point for investigation.

Librarians often consult the catalog as their primary source of information. Unfortunately, most nonfiction is currently cataloged only by subject and not by appeal elements such as language, pacing, or mood. To make matters worse, fiction—especially genre fiction—is sometimes not cataloged at all! But even when present in the catalog, brief genre entries do not necessarily facilitate the reader's search. For example, a request for "more contemporary romances set in Montana like Linda Lael Miller's Montana Creeds trilogy" is not facilitated by the brief genre entries "love stories" or "Montana," which are what most catalogs would offer.

The readers' advisor must also consider pacing, sensuality/violence/language, and the overarching themes of sibling rivalry, redemption, and reclaiming a proud heritage; some or all of these may be important to Miller's readers. The difficulty of relying on subject headings in order to construct read-alikes, or for general readers' advisory purposes, is ably discussed by Sarah Statz Cords in *The Real Story: A Guide to Nonfiction Reading Interests.*[9]

You should take into account the frame (setting, both in time and place; atmosphere) as well as the pacing, the genre, the narrative style, and the ways in which this author complies with (and stretches!) genre requirements. Take advantage of the questions and vocabulary lists generated by Joyce Saricks and the Adult Reading Round Table's Genre Studies web page to clarify the author's and individual titles' appeal to readers.[10]

Putting Pen to Paper

Now that you have established the appeal elements of your subject, author, or title, it is helpful to organize them and to write them out. In the NoveList model, several paragraphs are devoted to this examination, but in most cases where you merely want to provide the information to your readers, you can condense it into a short "shopping list" of attributes on which you plan to match other suggested titles or authors or both, or even a brief annotation. Decide how many titles you wish to offer as potential matches, and whether you must match them as closely as possible or whether you can offer a "stretch" title that is perhaps in a different genre or that covers another topic, but which nonetheless provides the more daring reader with a similar experience. As you write each annotation, remember to emphasize the elements that make the item a good match. Repeating the same vocabulary may run counter to your English teacher's advice, but repetition makes it much easier for your audience to pick up on similarities between items when they are scanning your list. For help with writing annotations, see chapter 6 of this book.

Now is the time to decide on your read-alike's format as well. You may choose to structure it as a bookmark, perhaps front-and-back using a three-column format, to be cut apart after printing. You may wish to include more titles than a bookmark can contain and to print the read-alike on a single page, to be posted on a bulletin board or shelf end cap or mounted in a binder with other read-alikes. Follow your creative instincts to create an attractive design, perhaps with the use of some graphics or an eye-catching shade of paper. It may be easiest to write all the annotations first and then arrange them according to "most similar" or alphabetically by author or in some other format. Nonfiction items may be grouped by call number or by any other organizational method that will make sense to your readers.

Readers new to this author or subject will benefit even more from your expertise if you remember to suggest a particular title as a good starting point. Often, readers are eager to explore something new but have no idea of the benchmark authors or what may be their best work. Encourage readers by listing a title that showcases the author's strengths.

Now that you understand how it's done, pick an author you enjoy and use the worksheet that follows this chapter to make some notes and create a read-alike list of your own!

NOTES

1. Joyce Saricks, *Readers' Advisory Service in the Public Library,* 3rd ed. (Chicago: American Library Association, 2005).

2. Joyce Saricks, *Readers' Advisory Guide to Genre Fiction,* 2nd ed. (Chicago: American Library Association, 2009).

3. Adult Reading Round Table, www.arrtreads.org.

4. Williamsburg Regional Library, "Looking for a Good Book?" www.wrl.org/bookweb/RA/; see also Wikipedia, "Readers' Advisory," http://en.wikipedia.org/wiki/Readers_advisory.

5. Fantastic Fiction, www.fantasticfiction.co.uk.

6. Kent District Library, "What's Next," www2.kdl.org/libcat/WhatsNextNEW.asp.

7. Reference and User Services Association, "The Reading List," www.ala.org/ala/mgrps/divs/rusa/awards/readinglist/index.cfm.

8. Phil Eskew, ed., "Bookmarks and Annotated Book Lists," http://ella.slis.indiana.edu/~pneskew/ra/booklists.html.

9. Sarah Statz Cords, *The Real Story: A Guide to Nonfiction Reading Interests,* ed. Robert Burgin (Westport, CT: Libraries Unlimited, 2006), xix.

10. Saricks, *Readers' Advisory Service in the Public Library,* chapter 3; Adult Reading Round Table, "Genre Studies," www.arrtreads.org/genrestudy.htm.

Author Read-Alike Worksheet

Author name(s) and website:

Resources used to compile the read-alike:

Genre(s) (if nonfiction, listing call numbers now will help you later):

Representative titles (list several and briefly describe or annotate; consider highlighting one, or one in each genre, as a good place to start; list the first title for each series and how many have been published to date in the series):

Elements that appeal to this author's readership:

Story themes

Character types

Language

Mood

Setting (time and place)

Author voice

Other author/title possibilities and the reasons/appeal factors that match:

Author #1 (include website)

Suggested title

Shared elements

Author #2 (include website)

Suggested title

Shared elements

Author #3 (include website)

Suggested title

Shared elements

Author #4 (include website)

Suggested title

Shared elements

Author #5 (include website)

Suggested title

Shared elements

Who Reads What?

Suspense	Thrillers	Action Adventure	Graphic Novels	Audiobooks
Fantasy	Science Fiction	Horror and Occult	Multicultural	Historical Fiction
Mystery: PI	Mystery: Cozy	Police Procedural	Forensic Mystery	Legal Mystery
Romance: Contemporary	Romance: Historical	Romance: Inspirational	Romance: Paranormal	Women's Lives
Gentle Reads	Western	Urban Fantasy	Chick Lit	Literary Fiction

Biography	Travel	History (General)	Microhistories	True Crime
Gardening	Back to the Land	Memoir	Cooking	Self-Help or Motivational
Natural History	Poetry	Sports	Politics	Environment
Cross-Genre (specify)	Other (specify)	Other (specify)	Other (specify)	Other (specify)

13

BOOK GROUP KITS

Lissa Staley

In addition to hosting book discussions, some libraries support book groups in their community by providing sets of books for discussion. In this chapter you will learn what book group kits contain, ideas for their reservation and circulation, and some of the benefits for creating book group kits for your community.

One predictor for whether people will return to a book discussion group the following meeting is the availability of the book title. Obtaining the book group selection can be a challenging process and a huge deterrent to the actual reading and enjoyment of the book to be discussed. For many people in book groups, time is wasted deciding if they want to buy the title or try to borrow it, remembering to look for the title, and waiting for the bookstore to special order the book or the library to request it. When they finally receive the book and get motivated to sit down and read it, they might not have enough time to finish it before their book group meets again. When members of a book group all rely on the local library to supply the next meeting's title, things can get competitive. After the new title is chosen, some patrons have been known to place discreet cell phone calls from the bathroom, trying to be the first to request the library's copy of the book.

By providing book group kits, the library can repackage its existing services to meet the unique needs of book groups. Book group attendees in your community are probably already using your library to check out a copy of the book or the movie version. They may use your databases to look up some background information on the author, go online to access and print out the discussion questions from the publisher's website, or even reserve a meeting room for their discussion. A book group kit can help consolidate these efforts, advertise complementary library services, and provide validation that reading and discussing books is a worthwhile activity.

CONTENTS OF THE KIT

At the most basic level, book group kits provide multiple copies of the same title. Eight to ten copies of a title should meet the needs of most book groups, but some libraries provide sets of up to twenty books.

In addition to the books, kits can contain supplements to facilitate or improve the discussion experience. Title-specific discussion questions are the most important addition and are often available from the publisher's website or collected on sites like ReadingGroupGuides.com. You could also include general book discussion questions and tips for leading book discussions in every kit. Libraries could offer to provide a facilitator for special discussions, like those in support of an annual community reading project.

Other supplementary materials can promote your library's collections, including related materials like large print or audio versions of the title, movie adaptations, or nonfiction history or travel books about the setting of the story. You might want to create a list of biographies of the author, other books by the same author, or recommended read-alikes. Another option is to publish an online resource page for each title, with links to books in your library catalog, articles in databases, online book reviews, and related websites. Because some book groups like to share food while they talk, consider including suggestions for related foods and recipes. Encourage patrons to add their own successful ideas before they return each kit.

Fancy packaging for book group kits is optional and depends on your budget and capacity for storage of assembled kits. Libraries have used zippered canvas bags, plastic tubs, plastic bags with handles, or recycled cardboard boxes. When choosing your packaging, consider if the kits will be shipped by courier, shared between branches, or interlibrary loaned to regional libraries.

If the entire kit will be checked out to the group leader, you can add conveniences like due date reminders and a sign-out sheet to help keep track of who has which individual copy. Also, you should list the replacement cost for individual lost books in case someone can't return a copy.

STARTUP COSTS

When proposing a book group kit collection for your library, it is helpful to estimate the costs for the initial collection. One basic kit might contain ten copies of a trade paperback title, which could be purchased for about $9 each with the standard discount from the library's supplier. You can order zippered canvas tote bags with a library logo imprint for about $8 each. Add a $2 binder to hold the discussion resources, and each kit will cost about $100 to create. If you use book sale donations or library discards to create your kits, this cost can be minimized.

Adding a single book on CD ($70) and a large print copy of the title ($30) can quickly double your cost per kit. In choosing book kit titles, it is important to consider the availability of large print titles and audiobooks, but patrons can still check out those alternate versions from the library's collection even if they aren't packaged with the book group kit.

CHOOSING TITLES

You will combine your readers' advisory and collection development skills when choosing book group kit titles. This collection carries an implicit endorsement from the library; the library promotes each of these books as worth reading and discussing. Some libraries create kits based on their library-sponsored discussion series, making the kits available for patron checkout after the library discussions have ended.

Choose popular discussable titles for your book group kits. Publishers and review sources will designate some titles as appropriate for book groups. You can also research which titles other libraries are discussing and ask for patron suggestions from established book groups. To gauge popularity, check ReadingGroupGuides.com, which ranks the most frequently requested reading guide titles.

Start your book group kit collection with several titles and add new titles each year if the collection is popular in your community. Not only does this expand your collection but it encourages your regular patrons to continue using the service by offering new selections for their groups. When selecting books, avoid stereotyping your book group patrons. They are not all middle-aged women, and even if they were, middle-aged women do not have uniform reading tastes. Remember that many people enjoy reading for a book group because of the challenge to read something different.

CIRCULATION PROCEDURES

How you choose to organize your book group kits, what to include, and how to circulate them will depend primarily on your library's unique situation. One method of circulation is not necessarily better than another; all options should be considered in context with your existing circulation procedures. Your book group kit collection may be subject to your library's existing policies regarding requests, interlibrary loan, courier service, overdue items, renewals, replacement or damage charges, level of cataloging, accessibility through the public catalog, customer suggestions for additional titles, and requests for reconsideration.

Creating a collection that will be useful to book groups involves understanding the dynamics of the book group calendar. For groups that meet monthly, a six-week checkout period can work well, although an eight- or nine-week checkout period would provide flexibility. Imagine this scenario: After the book group leader checks out a kit and distributes the books to her group, the members spend about a month reading the book in preparation for the discussion. The leader will reserve the second kit while the first is still checked out. Before the meeting to discuss the first book, the leader comes to the library to pick up the second kit and takes it to her book group meeting. She distributes copies of the second book to her group members, and everyone returns their copy of the first book to the leader, who returns the reassembled first book group kit to the library. If a member misses a meeting and doesn't return the book ahead of time, the leader may spend several days tracking down the missing book before returning the kit.

Given this already complicated situation, consider how you can make your book group kit experience easier for your patrons to use. If checkout periods and overdue fines are too restrictive, few groups will feel comfortable using the collection. If there are no consequences for overdue kits or for returning incomplete kits, the next patron's experience will suffer. Try to find a balance that works for your community and fits your library's circulation policies.

Reservations

Book group kits may be available on a walk-in basis, requested with a waiting list, or reserved in advance to guarantee a certain title at a certain time. Many book groups plan which titles they will read and discuss together. To meet the needs of those groups, I recommend allowing them to reserve their book group kits up to a year in advance if possible. When granting priority for reservations, consider favoring library-sponsored book groups, then book groups in your library's service area, over interlibrary loan requests. Individual details will depend on your circumstances.

Libraries currently circulating book group kits are using a wide variety of reservation systems. From paper-based calendars on a single employee's desk to Excel spreadsheets accessible to staff at multiple branches, reservation systems help staff plan ahead and ensure that particular kits are available at particular times to particular patrons. If you are lucky enough to be in a position to create a sophisticated online reservation system with patron-initiated requests and automated reports, remember that every system still has a librarian behind the scenes, checking that each kit contains the correct number of books and sending it out to the right person at the right time. Allow enough time between reservations to ensure the kit is returned, checked for missing books, restocked with handouts, and ready to be checked out to the next patron.

No Reservations

Reservations aren't for everyone. Some libraries cannot invest the staff time in keeping a reservation-based system running. Offering all the currently available book group kits on a shelf in the library still allows patrons to choose from a selection, but doesn't allow them to plan for particular titles. In a library system with branches, titles can be rotated through different locations to increase variation. Even if your library offers reservations, you may find that some patrons cannot seem to plan ahead. They want to walk in and pick out a kit immediately, or wait until the day of their book group meeting to call for a reservation. Offering a few "express kits" can help in this situation. You can use extra copies of books left over from previous community reading projects to create several kits that do not need to be reserved in advance. These kits are also useful for hand selling the larger book group kit collection, because a patron could take one that day to show the group members and gauge their interest about planning to use the collection in the future.

Another variation is useful if group leaders don't want to take responsibility for returning all the books in the kit. Instead of checking out the entire kit to one patron, some libraries hold the kit at the service desk during the reservation period and check out individual copies to patrons who ask for them. This model works well for library-sponsored book groups that are using book group kits to help provide enough copies for all group members.

ADVERTISING

Advertising the book group kit collection at your library is the best part. The kits relieve much of the stress associated with organizing book groups by providing a convenient assortment of resources tailored to hosting the discussion. Word of mouth is effective advertising as librarians recommend the collection to patrons who mention they are in book groups. A pamphlet or flyer can describe how to reserve or check out a kit and list the titles that your library provides. Promote the kits on the library's website and consider online reservations. Offering a library program on how to start a book group is a sneaky and effective way to promote this new collection and will attract interested patrons.

BENEFITS

Offering book group kits to your patrons encourages people to read and discuss books together. Similar to community reading projects, book group kits have the power to bring people together in conversation around books. An added bonus for the library is the opportunity to form relationships with local book group members and promote other library services.

If your library doesn't offer book group kits, you might access this type of collection for your library-sponsored group through a regional library system. In Kansas, for example, the state library compiles and updates a list of the book group kits that are available through interlibrary loan.

EXAMPLES

Book Discussion Sets at Park Ridge (Illinois) Public Library, http://book clubcorner.files.wordpress.com/2010/02/book-sets-owned-by-the-libraryweb.pdf: a list of titles for which the library has discussion sets

Book Club to Go, Siouxland Libraries, South Dakota, http://siouxland lib.org/adults/book_clubs/bookstogo.aspx: reservations via telephone and a simple informative site

Book Group in a Bag at Topeka and Shawnee County (Kansas) Public Library, www.tscpl.org/bgib/: blog-based website including online resource pages and reservations via an e-mail form

Book Club Kits at Santa Clara County (California) Library, www
.santaclaracountylib.org/services/lists/bookclubkit.html: online
guidelines for checkout and requests through the library catalog

Book Club Kits at Hennepin County (Minnesota) Library, www.hclib
.org/pub/bookspace/bookclubkit/index.cfm: online reservation
system

Book Discussion Group Sets Available in Kansas Libraries, http://sky
ways.lib.ks.us/KSL/libtech/bkdiscuss.html: various sets in a list
compiled for regional loans

14

TAKING READERS' ADVISORY ONLINE

Bobbi Newman

We're going to get a little bit technical in this chapter, but not too technical. Just enough so that even if you know next to nothing about website design, by the end of this chapter you will feel comfortable taking your readers' advisory services online.

At first glance, it can seem a little odd to consider providing readers' advisory services in the web zone, but so many aspects of readers' advisory can easily make the transition to an online service with little or no effort. Providing web-based RA help allows readers to access the service at their convenience day or night. It's more private, as no one can see the interaction between reader and advisor. In some cases it's even anonymous. Readers might be shy about approaching the public service desk, or they may not want others to know they are interested in a specific type of novel or subject. Creating access to online readers' advisory adds another great facet to library services.

When making the decision to put readers' advisory services online, libraries have many choices; ultimately all web-based assistance should serve the needs of the community. There are numerous ways to offer readers' advisory, and most of them fall into one of two categories—static or dynamic services. With static services the content is provided online, and it is up to the reader to seek it out and use it to the best of his or her ability. Other services are dynamic, customized suggestions in response to requests from individual readers. It is important to remember that online services should complement the service the library already provides. The staff time needed for creation and maintenance of these sites is a significant consideration. Libraries can implement a single type or multiple types of online readers' advisory services, but any online RA services should always be designed around what will work best for the library and its patrons.

Several tools allow libraries to provide online RA services. One option is to include readers' advisory services in a traditional website page; this will likely require assistance from the IT department each time a page needs to be updated. For librarians who want to make fast, easy changes themselves, blogs and wikis are great choices. Following are brief discussions of these options and some examples to help you decide which tool you would like to pursue. This chapter will focus on three types of online readers' advisory service: lists, forms, and book reviews. There are more, but these three are the most prevalent.

LISTS

One of the more traditional forms of service is the reading list. A library creates a list of titles that share a common theme, genre, character, time period, read-alike, subject based on repeated patron requests, and more (see chapters 10 and 11 in this book for guidance in creating lists). These lists are kept at the reference desk to be handed out to patrons. Print lists can be added to a library website fairly easily. Online lists have an advantage over printed lists: they can link the title directly to the library catalog. This feature allows the patron to see if the title is available, find out which library it is located in, and even place a hold. Many libraries already have print lists they have created over the years in response to reader demand. Adding these lists to the website can be one of the fastest and easiest ways to expand readers' advisory.

Once you have decided to add lists to your website, you need to decide what tool to use to make it happen. If you have the cooperation of the webmaster and the department in charge of website updates, you can incorporate the lists using whatever software the website is maintaining. If you will be doing the editing yourself, you might have to learn some new software. For libraries where library staff members do not have the access or the knowledge to easily create new content using traditional website building tools, blogs and wikis can be valuable options. Blogs and wikis generally require less technical knowledge and can allow multiple users to easily create and modify content. There are numerous free online services for both, as well as software options that can be installed and run locally, with assistance from the IT department. The benefit of using a blog or wiki is that creating content and publishing it is almost as simple as writing a Word document. If you're linking entries to the catalog, you will need to learn to make hyperlinks. Most services make these as simple as clicking a button and pasting the link.

Some Examples of Online Lists

The Missouri River (Missouri) Regional Library at one time created its lists using WordPress.org blogging software.[1] This software was installed on the library's server, so the lists were maintained and hosted locally. The lists contained call numbers and could be printed out. The titles also linked to the local catalog to make online reserving easier. You could duplicate this option using free web-hosted blogging software.

The Morton Grove (Illinois) Public Library lists are integrated into the library's website without links to the catalog.[2] Mid-Continent (Missouri) Public Library folds its lists into the library's website. Those lists contain a link to the local catalog but not a call number.[3]

The lists of the IRead Wiki, Iowa librarians' Readers' Advisory wiki, were created using a web-hosted wiki platform called PBworks.[4] PBworks has both free and paid options for service, and neither requires local installation. These lists do not link to a catalog or include a call number, but that can be done using a wiki. There are a number of free, web-hosted wiki platforms available to create this type of service.

Locally installed software makes it much easier to customize the look of the pages to match the rest of the library's website. However, even if you choose a service that is not hosted locally, you can still customize by adding the library's logo and matching the colors and layout whenever possible. Linking back and forth between the main site and the readers' advisory site or section will help integrate the readers' advisory services with the main site.

FORMS

Many libraries have paper forms that patrons can fill out to indicate their reading preference in many areas, including genre, tone, style, mood, age and gender of the main character, length of the book, recent books they enjoyed, and books they didn't like. A librarian then reviews the information and compiles a custom list for the reader. Most of these forms will easily make the transition to online service. After a readers' services staffer reviews the information and compiles the list, it can be sent to the patron via the preferred method indicated on the form, working much the same as a handwritten form would be processed. The forms vary from library to library, but all strive to give the advisor the information needed to make recommendations. When providing this type of readers' advisory it is important to let the reader know when he or she can expect to see the list and to assure the patron of the security of any submitted contact information.

Creation of online forms will require close work with IT or the webmaster to create and post the initial form. Submitted entry forms can then be delivered directly to the advisor via e-mail or stored in a database for the advisor to access. Williamsburg (Virginia) Regional Library and Salt Lake County (Utah) Library both have forms on their websites.[5]

BOOK REVIEWS

Library staff who want to take book reviews online will find that blogging software is the easiest option. Again, you have a choice between services that provide hosting for you and services that require local installation and hosting of content. Blogging software allows many authors to create and post reviews, each with his or her own login information. Online reviews can contain an image of the book cover along with the review and a link to the library's catalog to allow a patron to find the book. Reviews can be as short as a couple of sentences or as long as a couple of paragraphs (see chapter 6 in this book for guidance on writing book reviews).

Examples of Library Book Review Sites

Henderson (Nevada) District Public Libraries are using free online software to share book reviews, which include an image of the book jacket.[6] Madison (Wisconsin) Public Library is using locally installed and hosted software to post reviews.[7] Reviews include images of the book jacket and links back to the catalog.

Juneau (Alaska) Public Library is using free online software to share book reviews.[8] The reviews include book jacket images and link the titles to WorldCat.org.

BLOGS

Libraries can use blogs a number of different ways to communicate with and offer service to patrons. This section will focus on the readers' advisory uses. With blogs the line between the tool (or platform) and the service becomes blurred. A blog is a service *and* a tool. The software is the platform for the content, but that software allows something that is not really possible using some other platform. Blogs allow for multiple authors, each with a unique user name and password. As new content is created, the old content moves down the page and then on to the archives. You can easily add images and video clips. A blog can be used to share reviews, list recommendations, lead a discussion, pass along the announcement of award winners, or share recent additions to the library collections.

Blogs can be maintained using a number of free services that don't require local installation and staff time for maintenance. Of course, locally installed and hosted blogs can be customized to match the library's website. For example, Ann Arbor (Michigan) District Library incorporates its book blog and several other blogs into the front page of the library website.[9] Ann Arbor is using Drupal, a content management system, for its website and blogs. The Westport (Connecticut) Public Library is using Moveable Type, locally installed and hosted blogging software.[10] Newberg (Oregon) Public Library's Book Blog is using Blogger, a free service that doesn't require local software installation or hosting.[11]

PROMOTING YOUR ONLINE RA SERVICE

Now that you have put all that hard work into creating an online service, how do you get patrons to use it? Of course, there are the traditional ways libraries can announce a new service: flyers, posters, the local media, and so on. If you are still handing out paper lists, be sure they include a URL for the online service. For online advertisement, be sure you include links to the new readers' advisory service on several of your web pages. Additionally, link the readers' advisory pages back to the home page of the library website and to a few other choice pages, such as the catalog search or research page, so that users can move seamlessly around the website. You should also make sure staff members feel comfortable demonstrating and recommending the new service. Library staff who feel that a new service is great are more likely to promote it enthusiastically to patrons.

I know it can seem like taking readers' advisory online is a huge challenge, but if you take it one step at a time you will be comfortable with your online service very quickly. Your patrons will be thrilled with an additional service they can access from home, even when the library is closed.

NOTES

1. The Missouri River (Missouri) Regional Library, "What to Read Next," www.mrrl .org/blogs/wordpress/books/ (retrieved November 2009).

2. Morton Grove (Illinois) Public Library, "The Fiction_L Booklists," www.webrary .org/rs/FLbklistmenu.html.

3. Mid-Continent (Missouri) Public Library, "Based on the Book," www.mcpl.lib .mo.us/readers/movies/.

4. IRead Wiki, "Welcome to IRead Wiki, Iowa librarians' Readers' Advisory wiki," http://iread.pbworks.com.

5. Williamsburg (Virginia) Regional Library, "Looking for a Good Book?" www.wrl .org/bookweb/RA/index.html; Salt Lake County (Utah) Library, "Personalized Booklist," www.slco.lib.ut.us/booksnmore/personal_booklist.htm.

6. Henderson (Nevada) District Public Libraries, "Novel News," http://hdplnovel news.blogspot.com.

7. Madison (Wisconsin) Public Library, "MADreads," www.madisonpubliclibrary .org/madreads/.

8. Juneau (Alaska) Public Library, "Juneau Public Library Blog," http://juneaubook blog.wordpress.com.

9. Ann Arbor (Michigan) District Library, www.aadl.org.

10. Westport (Connecticut) Public Library, "Westport Public Library Book Blog," www.westportlibrary.org/bookblog/.

11. Newberg (Oregon) Public Library, "Newberg Public Library Book Blog," http:// nplbookblog.blogspot.com.

Part 4

Programming

15

BOOK GROUPS

Kay Sodowsky

At its best, a book discussion group can be a work of art. Like a great painting that reveals its secrets layer by layer, or a live performance that brings you almost to tears, the act of gathering with other readers and sharing insights gleaned from the written word has the potential to be profoundly rewarding.

Like all great endeavors a book group also has the potential to fail miserably. An uncomfortable environment, poor book choice, or lack of preparation on the part of the moderator can all contribute to a lackluster experience. Add one or more troublesome attendees and your group is sure to lose some members before the next meeting. This chapter is not intended to be a comprehensive guide to book groups; the goal is to offer a ready reference tool that's accessible, practical, and fun to read.

TERMINOLOGY

Persons who assume responsibility for book discussion groups wear many hats and use a wide range of titles to denote their role. In many settings, the book group leader is simply "the librarian." Personally, I dislike the term *leader* because I conceptualize book groups as an egalitarian meeting of minds, and *leader* suggests someone to whom the others defer. I prefer the title *moderator* and envision myself as an unobtrusive traffic cop who gently steers the discussion. In the academic world, the term *facilitator* is often used to indicate the person responsible for guiding a discussion. If book groups are held in private homes, then *host* is certainly apt. There is no right or wrong choice; use whatever title feels appropriate for you.

Please note that when the term *librarian* is used I'm referring to any library employee who is tasked with the responsibility of moderating a book group. Many wonderful book groups have been created and maintained by library paraprofessionals or by friends of the library.

ORGANIZING AND STRUCTURING A NEW BOOK GROUP

When it comes to starting a new book discussion group, one size does not fit all. What works in one library may not be a good fit for another group. Librarians often approach new book groups with a kind of "We can do this!" enthusiasm, then realize that they failed to consider both the needs of their audience and their own style as a moderator. Carefully assess the expectations and needs of your potential readers, plus your own preferences, and plan accordingly.

1. Survey your target audience.
   a. When can they attend?
   b. What do they want from a book discussion group?
   c. See sample 1 at the end of this chapter.
2. Using the survey results, decide on basic meeting parameters.
   a. When (evening, afternoon, weekend), where (library, restaurant, private home), and how often (monthly, bimonthly, quarterly, "special occasion" or one time only)?
   b. Food or no food? Coffee or no coffee?
   c. Brown-bag meetings? Will the library provide beverage(s)?
   d. How will books be obtained and distributed? Talk to your ILL department to make sure you're all on the same page about ordering multiple copies for groups.
   e. Adults-only group or all ages welcome?
3. Define the structure for your meetings.
   a. *Low* structure: no moderator and no formal questions. People just talk. Meeting ends when people stop talking.
   b. *Medium-low* structure: rotating moderator. Moderator du jour decides how to conduct meeting.
   c. *Medium-high* structure: librarian moderator. Librarian does background research, develops questions, and moderates the discussion. Discussion lasts sixty to ninety minutes.
   d. *High* structure: shared inquiry method (the Great Books Foundation)

4. Select your meeting format.
   a. Librarian/moderator does research and asks questions.
   b. Rotating moderator decides for each meeting.
   c. Eat first, talk later.
   d. Eat and discuss simultaneously (brown-bag session).
   e. Tag-team approach—one person does background research on author and another writes questions. Take turns asking questions.
   f. Hand out discussion questions in advance so readers can think about the discussion topics while reading the book.
   g. Limit meeting to just book discussion *or* include extra time for booktalks and roundtable sharing of individual members' reading.

ONE-TIME-ONLY EVENTS AND THEME DISCUSSIONS

If you're not willing to commit to a recurring book group, consider hosting a one-time-only book discussion as a special occasion event or as a tie-in with other thematic programming. Special occasion discussions can focus on any number of topics.

Author
- best-selling author
- local author
- children's author also of interest to adults for a Family Night Book Discussion

Event/Holiday (use Chase's Calendar of Events *to identify other events)*
- famous person's birthday
- Black History Month/Women's History Month
- Earth Day
- Disability Awareness Month

Current events/Seasonal
- world or national affairs
- sports
- movie tie-in

Cooperative event with another organization
- baseball book discussion—attendees get a free ticket to a baseball game

- historical book—attendees get free admission to a local museum
- movie tie-in—readers earn passes to a film screening

MARKETING YOUR BOOK GROUP

1. Promote the book group to your internal audience of library patrons and coworkers.
   a. Create flyers.
   b. Advertise in your library newsletter.
   c. Post information on the library web page.
   d. Display posters at the circulation desk.
2. Reach out to your external audience.
   a. Send press releases to area newspapers.
   b. List your group on the local cable TV community bulletin board.
   c. Send flyers to other libraries for posting.
3. For thematic discussions, identify local organizations and invite them to attend.
   a. Consider partnering with organizations such as veterans groups, disability support groups, author fan clubs, local writing groups, or college multicultural clubs.
   b. Invite another existing book group to join you for a joint meeting.
4. If you want to see a big jump in attendance, select and advertise a book for a popular "cult author" like Stephenie Meyer.
   a. You'll have a big crowd and a great discussion.
   b. Attendees probably won't be back unless you do another book by that same author.

BOOK SELECTION: HERE'S WHERE IT GETS INTERESTING!

Book selection is important, although a skilled moderator can turn even a bad book into a good discussion. But with so many wonderful books to discuss, why not select one worthy of your time?

1. Who selects the books?
   a. The moderator
   b. Group members, who nominate titles

    c. Others (e.g., Oprah's books, award winners)

    d. The omnipotent library person who hosts the group (if not already the moderator)

2. Consider availability, format, and your members' preferences; try to be as inclusive as possible.

    a. Should you only read books available in paperback? Hardcover books may be too heavy for readers with physical disabilities.

    b. If you read current best sellers, how will you get enough copies?

    c. Do any of your members require large print books or audiobooks?

    d. If you allow members to suggest titles, what do you do if a member insists on reading a particular book but the book is too new, too ancient, or too obscure to be readily obtained?

3. How long is the book?

    a. Ideal length for a discussion title is 250–400 pages.

    b. If under 200 pages, consider doing two smaller books to compare and contrast. Paired books can illustrate different treatments of the same subject; consider the portrayal of mental illness in *The Bell Jar* compared to *Girl, Interrupted.*

    c. If over 400 pages, allow extra time between meetings; if the group takes a holiday or summer break, you might pick a longer book for reading over the break.

    d. Alternate long books with shorter books so slower readers can finish assigned books at least half of the time.

4. What about series books or genre reading?

    a. Assign the first book of the series unless you're sure a sequel can stand alone and still be enjoyable.

    b. A mystery or literary science fiction title will work, but be careful about romance or westerns unless you're certain that book group members will read in these genres.

5. Know your group when considering

    a. Fiction versus nonfiction—be clear on how much of each will be read when the group is formed; use your survey results. Members with a strong preference will be dismayed if the reading list turns out different from what they expected.

    b. Male authors versus female authors (alternate as much as possible)

    c. American authors, British authors, or international authors

    d. "Sensitive readers" (graphic sexual content, violence, or language)

    e. The "yuck factor"—topics that might cause your readers to reject the book outright. Will members of your group stay home rather than discuss female circumcision in *Possessing the Secret of Joy*?

6. Consider the following when selecting nonfiction:

    a. Look for readable and accessible titles versus scholarly treatments.

    b. Nonfiction should be of interest to a general audience.

    c. Read reviews and watch best-seller lists to identify readable nonfiction authors.

    d. Nonfiction may attract more men to a book group.

    e. When discussing nonfiction, it's not necessary to be an expert on the subject. You're discussing a single book, not the entire Civil War. If your research discovers reviews that criticize the accuracy of the book, then bring that up in the discussion.

7. What about character versus plot? Whether fiction or nonfiction, good books for discussion tend to focus on the characters, not on the plot. For example, fast-paced thrillers don't usually have well-developed characters and might leave reading groups with little to discuss.

8. More book selection tips:

    a. Seek out annotated reading lists. Although the list is dated, I return to *What to Read?* by Mickey Pearlman again and again.[1]

    b. Ellen Moore and Kira Stevens offer a very comprehensive annotated bibliography of book group resources in *Good Books Lately*.[2]

    c. Network with library colleagues to get book recommendations and to share best practices; view other libraries' web pages to see what their groups are reading.

    d. Have broad reading tastes and keep an eye out for books that *you* feel the need to discuss. If you're just dying to talk to someone about a particular book, then chances are it's a good discussion group title.

    e. Consider the sensitivities of individual group members, but don't reject a title just because you suspect that one person will be offended by the book.

    f. The best discussions happen when members disagree about a book. If everyone adores the book, then the discussion is likely to be short.

BEFORE THE MEETING: RESEARCH!

A dedicated moderator will do enough background research before the group meets to be able to provide author information and context for the book. Research allows the moderator to write good questions and to anticipate reader reaction.

- Use print and online reference tools to find information on the author, including biographical details and insight into her or his writing process. Groups tend to psychoanalyze the author; in the absence of factual data, they will invent their own "mythology" about the author's motives and background instead of focusing on the book itself.

- Find book reviews, both positive and negative.

- Print online reading guides from publisher websites. (Google the title and "reading guide" to locate.)

- Skim through reader comments on Amazon.com for a snapshot of how other readers react to this book.

- Locate nonfiction materials related to the setting and themes in the book.

- Identify fiction read-alikes.

- Find any film adaptations of the book. If it's currently being made into a film, which actors have been cast?

- Look up any terms you don't know from the book or from reviews.

WRITING QUESTIONS

New moderators sometimes agonize over writing discussion questions. Relax, it gets much easier over time!

- Adjust questions to your group's strengths and weaknesses. If your folks tend to lose focus and go off on tangents, ask fairly specific questions (e.g., "How did Billy's childhood influence the decisions he made after the accident?" instead of "So, what did you think of Billy?").

- Organize your questions so that discussion will flow naturally, but be flexible enough to rearrange questions on the fly.

- Focus on characterization; whether fictional characters or real persons, everyone makes choices. Talk about these choices. Why did this person behave this way? Was this situation handled in a believable manner?

- Quote a review, the more outrageous the better, and say, "One critic said this about the book. Do you agree or disagree?" Everyone likes to argue with the critics!

- Use reading group guides from publishers to stimulate your thinking, but be careful about using questions verbatim from the guides. Some of these suggested questions are more suitable for a college-level English literature course than a library book discussion.

WHAT DO PEOPLE DISCUSS IN READING GROUPS?

No matter how the questions are worded, the same basic themes will appear in every book discussion. Once you begin to examine books with an eye toward moderating discussions of them, these basic themes will quickly reveal themselves as possible questions for the group. In *The Reading Group Handbook,* Rachel Jacobsohn identifies topics that provoke the most discussion:[3]

characters and story line	literary merit
characters' actions	work's similarity to other readings
social implications	narrative style
symbolism	theme
author's purpose	point of view, style, setting
credibility/believability	concept of self
emotional response of reader	concept of God
personal experiences of reader	concept of time and memory
plot resolution	

SETTING THE MOOD: MAKE IT FUN! "CELEBRATE" THE BOOK!

Whether you're promoting a new reading group or attempting to enliven an existing group, it's always fun to inject whimsical touches that relate to the title under discussion. Unleash your creative muse and celebrate the book!

1. Have appropriate background music playing when group members arrive.
   a. *Memoirs of a Geisha*—Japanese music
   b. *Angela's Ashes*—Irish folk songs
   c. *Wasn't That a Time?*—recordings of FDR's speeches or fireside chats
   d. *Truman*—recordings of Truman's speeches

2. Display read-alikes nearby.
   a. Include any other books by the author.
   b. If the book is in a series, have the next title in the series ready for checkout.
   c. Place topical books on the table for persons who want to read more about the subject, especially if the books have been referenced in the title being discussed.
      i. *Ashley Book of Knots*—a must when discussing *The Shipping News*
      ii. Ansel Adams's book of Manzanar photos for *Farewell to Manzanar*
      iii. Mexican cookbooks for *Like Water for Chocolate*
      iv. *Dictionary of British English* when reading British works
      v. books about foreign customs when discussing international fiction
      vi. books of quilt patterns for *How to Make an American Quilt* and *Alias Grace*
      vii. books about Bleeding Kansas (with photos of historical characters) for *The All-True Travels and Adventures of Lidie Newton*

3. Show photographs of real-life persons who appear in historical fiction titles.

4. Provide assorted visual aids—maps are important when the setting is integral to the story.
   a. Map of Newfoundland for *The Shipping News*
   b. Map of the San Juan Islands for *Snow Falling on Cedars*
   c. Photo of an Aga stove if you have British characters sitting in front of the Aga

    d. *King Lear* outline to compare to the family in *A Thousand Acres*

    e. Mah-jongg tiles for *The Joy Luck Club*

5. Display travel souvenirs to highlight a special setting.

    a. Brochures from John Adams's home in Quincy, Massachusetts, for *John Adams*

    b. Tour brochures and postcards from Savannah for *Midnight in the Garden of Good and Evil*

    c. Coins from relevant foreign countries

6. Add small whimsical touches to draw attention to a character or theme.

    a. Serve water in blue cups while discussing *The Widows' Adventures* in which one of the characters sips beer from a blue cup throughout the story.

    b. For *Fast Food Nation*, serve water in McDonald's courtesy cups with napkins from Wendy's and Burger King.

    c. Serve small snacks related to the theme or setting of the book.

7. Be outrageous.

    a. Show up dressed appropriately for the setting of the book. Excavate your closets for a fez, a Hawaiian shirt, a sombrero, a trench coat suitable for a spy, a poodle skirt, and so on.

    b. Decorate the meeting room with dinosaur décor for *Jurassic Park*.

    c. Dress up your well-behaved dog as a character from the book (caution: not advised for cats).

WHAT ABOUT THE MOVIE?

When a book is made into a film, readers will understandably be curious about how the book translates to the screen. People who have seen the film version often try to discuss the plot of the film instead of the book. Steer the comments back to the book by offering to let them talk about the movie at the end of the meeting. You might also consider incorporating the film into the discussion:

- Show a five- to ten-minute clip of an intense or pivotal scene.
- If your library owns the DVD, have it ready for checkout. Even if you don't show a clip, people will want to see the film.
- Consider showing a clip from a documentary to illustrate something essential to your book's setting or theme.

TIPS FOR BEING A GOOD BOOK GROUP MODERATOR

1. Strive to be nonjudgmental and welcome all comments; do not allow anyone to dismiss someone else's opinions as invalid or stupid. Make it clear that all comments and opinions will be respected.

2. Reserve your opinions about the book until everyone else has spoken.

3. *Listen* to all comments and paraphrase; use comments to segue into another question.

4. Gently steer the discussion in a logical and orderly direction without being aggressive and authoritarian. Be subtle!

5. Discourage side conversations; it's very distracting to have two people talking between themselves and especially discouraging for members with hearing problems who will feel slighted. If someone on one end of the table doesn't hear what's been said, repeat the comment or ask the speaker to talk a bit louder.

6. It isn't usually a great idea to call on people and force them to talk. If someone wants to attend but not speak, that's okay. However, encourage comments and ask a talkative person to "hold that thought" if a shy person is attempting to speak. Don't let the shy person's comments get talked over or ignored by the more articulate members who may talk quickly and more forcefully.

7. If quiet people are in the majority, try a nonthreatening question like "If this book were made into a film, what actor would you cast as the main character?" then go around the circle. This question is a good icebreaker, because there's no right or wrong answer.

CHALLENGES FOR MODERATORS

What do you do when a book group attendee just sucks the joy right out of the room? Unless you're confident that you have the skills to react quickly when weirdness erupts, it's worth thinking in advance about difficult situations and how you might want to respond. Every experienced book group moderator has stories to tell about moments when she or he just wanted to crawl under the table. Consider how you might respond if you encounter any of the following. Thinking about these situations in advance will help moderators be and feel more prepared when these characters show up.

- Mrs. Hostile, who hates every book and berates you in front of the group whether you're the one who selected the book or not.
- Mr. Loquacious and Mrs. Know-It-All, who monopolize the discussion.
- Ms. Nutjob, who goes off on wild rants about topics minimally related to the book.
- Mrs. Weepy, who interjects the details of her abandonment and recent (or not so recent) divorce into every discussion.
- Mr. and Ms. Procrastinator, who never finish a book before the meeting.
- Miss Single, who drags her boyfriend to the meeting even though he hasn't read the book (which doesn't deter him from jumping into the discussion).
- Mrs. Racist, who doesn't like African American writers because she says that blacks are lazy and are always "whining" about their situation.
- Mr. Lonely Widower, who's cruising for a new wife.
- Ms. Doting Parent, who brings her child to the adult book group. May come in two versions: precocious child who actually read the book *or* child who doesn't have a clue what's going on or why he's there. Can we go home now?

UNTIL NEXT TIME

- Remind everyone of the date for the next meeting and the title of the next book.
- Have copies of the next book available for checkout.
- Keep a log of books you've done and how the discussion went.
- Once a year, give group members a cumulative bibliography of all the books that have been discussed to give them (and you!) a sense of accomplishment.

CONCLUSION

After nearly two decades of working with book discussion groups as a founder, a moderator, and an attendee, I continue to be excited by the proliferation of book discussion groups in all their many guises. As a librarian, I have a deeply felt affection for library reading groups and for the libraries that look upon their reading groups as a core service to their communities. In the context of readers' advisory, what better way to enrich the lives and minds of our patrons than to share our mutual connection with the magic of the written word? Now, go forth and discuss!

NOTES

1. Mickey Pearlman, *What to Read: The Essential Guide for Reading Group Members and Other Book Lovers,* rev. ed. (New York: Harper, 1999).
2. Ellen Moore and Kira Stevens, *Good Books Lately* (New York: St. Martin's, 2004), 331–345.
3. Rachel W. Jacobsohn, *The Reading Group Handbook,* rev. ed. (New York: Hyperion, 1998), 125–137.

16

HOW TO HOST AUTHOR EVENTS

Paul Smith

Libraries could not exist without those authors who keep packing the shelves with the latest and greatest nonfiction and fiction books. So it is hardly surprising that libraries make great forums for contemporary writers to meet their readers and recruit new readers through public events. Public events can vary widely—including panel discussions, exhibit openings, film screenings, live music, and other performance events. Every kind of event has its own unique challenges. However, the author event is the most common denominator—a public event that any library can organize successfully. This chapter will focus on author events intended for adult audiences; the most successful events for young audiences generally incorporate a performance element (such as the Junie B. Jones Stupid Smelly Bus Tour) that makes these activities a completely different animal.

GETTING STARTED

The importance of public programming should be clearly acknowledged before planning an event. In particular, any library employee whose primary responsibility is not public programming needs authorization to assist with or devise public programming—and that authorization should indicate how many hours each week the employee(s) should devote to public programming. A library that hosts one or two events per year could likely get by with a small committee (no more than five members) that meets regularly (weekly), provided each member is active and has well-defined responsibilities. A library that hosts one or two events per week needs (at the least) a programming coordinator. A library that hosts several events per week needs a programming department. All public programming should enhance the image of the library: do not undermine that goal by pursuing a project that is too grand or that requires excessive time to organize.

All public programming benefits from a systematic approach that is based on clear goals. Examples of quantifiable goals include attracting a target number of patrons to a specific event or a series of events; bringing a new demographic or niche audience into the library; boosting circulation numbers by a specific percentage or within a specific genre; increasing Friends of the Library membership; or achieving a certain number of media hits or impressions. Clear goals require clear communication. No planning or logistics conversation should proceed without a note taker, and all e-mails should be saved for reference. Notes and e-mails can be lifesavers—or at least face savers. If public programming is a common activity, devise standard procedures and checklists to help manage responsibilities and ensure that all essential details are considered. Revisit and revise these forms often.

ASSESS YOUR STRENGTHS

When approaching public programming, evaluate those unique qualities that could strengthen the competitive advantage of your library. All libraries share one unique quality that separates them from other public institutions and arts organizations that might be public programming competitors: libraries attract readers—and by patronizing their libraries, these readers take a piece of that institution with them into their homes. This is why the author event is the most common denominator.

A museum cannot send a part of its collection home with its visitors. The opera and the theater and the rock concert make great memories but offer few tangibles—and none that is free. Book circulation can further public programming goals by: drawing readers to a central location (the circulation desk) where event notification(s) can be posted; serving as convenient vehicles for event promotional items (a bookmark or postcard that details the upcoming event) placed inside by circulation staff; serving as a barometer for what your reading population is most interested in—and thus suggesting a natural audience for an event that complements a popular genre or topic or author.

But your library may possess other strengths as well, such as a unique facility or space within your building—perhaps a room that can accommodate a particularly large crowd; or a unique personnel asset, perhaps a gifted outreach librarian or web designer who can spread word of your event out into the community or cyberspace.

FUNDING

Public programming costs money—ranging from a few hundred dollars (for events focused on local authors or local history) to tens of thousands (for events featuring major personalities: if a speakers' bureau is involved, your budget will need some zeros). The total bill even for a series of low-cost programs moves quickly into the thousands, so an early priority should always be to establish a funding source and a budget. Beyond your library budget (or lack thereof), there are plenty of opportunities for funding public programs. It is essential to have money in hand or in the bank: do not start a project with the mere promise of funding, which could be redirected or withheld. An even worse scenario is that the manager or donor of the money uses its promise as leverage to change the plan and muddle the established objectives. Public grants are a valuable funding source, and the options abound: the American Library Association and Public Library Association offer an array of grant opportunities, as do the National Endowment for the Arts and the National Endowment for the Humanities as well as local, state, and regional arts agencies. Private grants can be equally valuable though potentially more difficult to find or access. Local or national trusts, foundations, or endowments—even philanthropic or charitable organizations—can be sources for grants. Friends of the Library groups can also fund public programming by directing membership contributions to this purpose or by holding fund-raisers.

PARTNERS

Programming partners can reduce or share costs associated with an event or provide in-kind services. A good partner can also benefit a public program by providing any of the following: the author (through personal connections or financial resources, or perhaps the partner is the actual author who donates his or her time out of goodwill or desire for exposure); the venue (especially if your library lacks a facility); catering (provided your event would benefit from appetizers and drinks); promotional help (in the form of designing printed or online packages—or by covering these costs); and books or book sales (enter the bookstore as partner).

A partner or partners can provide much-needed assistance. However, there is a trade-off: instead of working for your own established goals, the partner organization often brings its own set of goals into the project. Furthermore, an unhappy partner can undermine an event—so by accepting a partnership, you are inviting into the fold a new group of people who must be at least satisfied with the experience.

BOOKING THE AUTHOR

Based on your programming objectives, select a few potential authors who would best facilitate these goals. Book tours, family life, and teaching commitments often present scheduling challenges, so it is always best to have more than one author or multiple dates in mind. The next step is to gauge the interest and availability of the author. If the author is local, this can sometimes be as simple as picking up the phone. If the author has a national reputation, prepare to work through intermediaries—publicists and other handlers who work for the author's publishing house: pick up a copy of her latest work in order to determine the publishing house and where to start, or check the author's website for contact and booking information.

In this initial pitch to the author or her representative, present your vision of the event—one that will hopefully prove equally inspiring to the author. Describe anything that might catch her attention, be it the event space, the marketing plan, or the dedicated audiences that have attended previous events. For example, I once presented an event concept to an author who waived a five-figure speaking fee because the concept was so appealing. In short: a compelling pitch pays. In these preliminary conversations, be sure to state clearly your expectations for a public event: if there is a particular book or even a particular topic or theme that you want addressed, state this plainly and repeat this expectation frequently. Propose a title for the event that leaves no doubt.

Before making a final decision, take into account such factors as an author's voice and physical presentation as well as any interest and availability in working with local media. Previous radio or television interviews featuring the author—even a simple phone conversation—can be instructive. When booking a local author, sometimes a simple e-mail exchange with all the terms, such as payment (if any), travel arrangements, and media availability, set in writing will suffice. A nationally best-selling author may require a formal contract.

THE BASICS

In the actual event planning stage, the basics consist of date and time and place—and nothing is more potentially destructive than getting this information jumbled or confused. Once an agreement is reached with the author, send a blanket e-mail with these basics to all parties involved in the planning and execution of the event—and triple-check the basics to ensure that they are correct.

Date. Avoid holidays. If your community is particularly religious, consider avoiding religious holidays. Avoid scheduling events on days when daylight saving time comes into effect: there will always be some folks who miss the time change. Be aware of your surroundings and competitors: if your classical music presentation is competing (intentionally or not) with the professional orchestra's debut of a new composition, you will lose.

Time. There are few hard-and-fast rules regarding the time selected for a program. Just consider that 2 p.m. on a Thursday is much different than 2 p.m. on a Sunday, especially if you are hosting events consistently and wish to build a loyal audience. It is also advisable to work with standard event start times in order to eliminate confusion: if one event begins at 6 p.m. on Wednesday and another begins at 6:30 p.m. the next day, you will keep your audience guessing—but in exactly the wrong aspect.

Place. Make certain your event space is not double-booked. Publish the address for your event space in all promotional items for the event. Make certain that your event space is suitable for the program: do not screen a film or attempt to project a PowerPoint in a room with a solid wall of windows without blinds in the afternoon.

AUDIOVISUAL COMPONENTS

Technology can significantly improve an event in myriad ways. For instance, it is highly recommended that your author speak with a microphone—not everyone in your audience will have excellent hearing, and those in the back of a room may need the sonic boost that a microphone can provide. PowerPoint presentations are also fairly common and require a screen, a projector, a computer, and sometimes sound output as well. In short: ask your author about his plans for AV components early. If you cannot accommodate AV components, state this at the outset. Your event will go much more smoothly if you plan for AV components at the start. Your event will go even more smoothly if an AV tech (likely someone from your IT department) can be on-site to assist with the program.

RSVPS

The following discussion is predicated on the notion that your event is free and open to the public—that there is no ticket issued or fee charged for participation in the event. The vast majority of public events will benefit from coordinating a system to collect RSVPs. Otherwise all your preparations are pure guesswork. Ideally, your RSVP system should dump all information into a centralized electronic database that includes (at a minimum) the patron name, phone number or e-mail address or both (to be used either for RSVP reminders or in case of a cancellation), and the number of seats requested. It is possible to set up an electronic database that collects both RSVPs taken by phone and RSVPs submitted online. Be aware: if you accept only phone RSVPs, you are catering to a demographic that generally predates the Internet; if you accept only online RSVPs, you are catering only to a younger, Internet-savvy demographic while excluding those on the wrong side of the digital divide.

Asking for RSVPs is an effective gauge of public interest in an event. The public is by definition a diverse group that will surprise you by what does and does not elicit its response. By scheduling an event without seeking any indication of public response, you are walking blindly into that event: without RSVPs, you might prepare for fifty attendees only to see five show up—which amounts to a lot of wasted effort. In my experience, an RSVP system will generally get you within 10 percent of your real audience four out of five times.

Also be aware of the meaning of *RSVP*, which comes from the French, *répondez s'il vous plaît*, meaning "Please reply." An RSVP does not guarantee a patron a seat. An RSVP for five people does not ensure that these five people will be able to sit together, particularly in a packed house. An RSVP does not preclude a standing room only event. It is merely a tool to aid you in planning, and it is in the best interest of the patrons to provide that RSVP if they want a satisfactory experience—and it is in your best interest to encourage them to make that RSVP.

AUTHOR READINGS

Here shall be taken up the eternal debate: whether an author should read aloud from her work during an event. Like all great debate questions, both sides have a compelling case. The affirmative side can argue that an author reading can be a compelling introduction to her work for those in the audience who are unfamiliar with it and came out of curiosity—and this same reading can also offer unique insights for the seasoned reader and devoted fan, who will be inspired to reconsider the author and her work as a result. The negative side would respond by arguing that not all authors make good readers—that, in fact, it is rare to find an author who is an accomplished reader. The affirmative side could not refute this. The negative side would also offer the following bit of wisdom: some adults do not like to be read aloud to—and those who do sometimes fall asleep.

If possible, the author event should focus on something apart from a simple reading: ask the author to discuss the historical or social context of his work, the inspiration for the story or for certain characters, the research process—even a simple explanation of the book without directly reading from it. Perhaps a local university professor would lead an interview-style discussion with the author. However, some authors simply cannot be dissuaded from reading aloud from their own works: if an author insists, simply request that he read for no more than five minutes at a time. Among the downsides to a poetry event is that there is generally no choice aside from the straight reading—but in these cases, always encourage the poet to give each poem an introduction and an afterword.

EVENT FLOW

The flow of the event is also important—and if your library will be hosting public events regularly, the flow of events should also be standardized as much as possible so that patrons know what to expect. A foolish consistency is more than just the hobgoblin of little minds; it is also the sign of an event host who understands the importance of making the public feel at ease within its space.

Depending on the event, give yourself at least an hour to start preparing the event space before your audience arrives—and they will generally start arriving thirty minutes prior. If a large crowd is expected or there are any unfamiliar or unusual components to the event, start preparations much earlier. All told, an event (from its formal beginning to its eventual end) will take at least ninety minutes. The event staff will invest at least twice that much time. The event flow should include the following: an RSVP check-in table, a five-minute delay, an introduction, the author presentation, a Q&A session, closing remarks, and book signing.

> If you have opted to collect RSVPs, you should set up a table (staffed
> by either library staff members or volunteers) where attendees
> should check in—allowing you to gauge the value of those RSVPs

that have been collected while reinforcing the notion that respond-
ing is important. For those attendees who have not responded,
a card should be offered that would allow the library to collect
name and contact information in order to send promotional material regarding future events. In addition to collecting information
about RSVPs, this check-in table provides an immediate contact
with your guests, allowing them to ask questions about the event
and receive information about future events.

The five-minute delay is simply a good idea: if your event is
scheduled for 6:30 p.m., wait until 6:35 p.m. to begin. This gap
allows your stragglers and those folks battling unexpected traffic
and parking delays a bit of extra time so that they do not miss
anything.

A representative from your library should generally introduce the
author. Especially if you are in a venue outside your library, a
formal introduction will reinforce the fact that this is a library
event and give members of the audience a face to connect with
the library so that if they have questions or compliments after
the event, the audience members know whom to approach.

The author presentation is the main event—and for all intents and
purposes, it is out of your hands. In arranging this event, you
can ask that the author speak on a certain topic, refrain from
reading aloud, and use the provided microphone—but once the
author takes the stage, she will do what she wants. It is never
advisable to pull someone off the stage in order to cajole her
into sticking to the agreed-upon terms, so all you can do is hope
that she likes you enough to go along with the plan. A forty-
five-minute presentation should be the target: a thirty-minute
presentation is generally not enough time for much substance;
a sixty-minute presentation is acceptable but will inspire seat
squirming; anything beyond an hour is not advised.

The Q&A session presents unique issues and is discussed at length in
the following section.

Closing remarks should generally follow the Q&A session. At this
point, the library representative who introduced the author
should return to the stage, shake hands with the presenter,
and thank him for a lovely presentation, followed by a quick
reminder about the book sales/signing or a plug for another
upcoming event.

The book signing may require flexibility and is also discussed at
length in a later section.

QUESTION-AND-ANSWER SESSIONS

There is no good way to facilitate a question-and-answer session. Here are
a few options, each paired with its accompanying problem.

In scenario one, neither the questioner nor the author has a microphone. The problem: some if not most of the audience will not
be able to hear or understand either the question or the answer,
and this segment of the audience will become annoyed and
might just start yelling, "Speak up!" Some attendees may leave
prematurely.

In scenario two, the author has a microphone and she has been
instructed to repeat every question before answering. The
problem: the author will inevitably forget to repeat the questions—she may not even remember to repeat the first one—
leading to the same result just described.

In scenario three, the questioner is provided a microphone (dutifully
carried around the room by an accommodating library staff
member), and the author has a microphone. The problem: it is
always dangerous to give a microphone to a person you are not
familiar with—Q&A sessions usually include a small population
that will ask a totally unrelated or belligerent question, or both,
and a larger population of individuals who will precede their
question about the novel with a novella-length preamble (or
pre-ramble). Once you hand someone a microphone, it belongs
to him until he gives it back. There is the additional problem
that some questioners may not wait for the accommodating staff
member to hand them the microphone and will simply shout out
their questions, leading to the same results described earlier.

In scenario four, the questioner walks to a microphone placed on a
microphone stand in a central location to pose the question. The
problem: essentially the same as described in scenario three.

In scenario five, the library event staff hands out question cards
along with writing implements to event attendees and instructs
them to write their questions on the cards, which are then
collected prior to the Q&A session—the library event staff then
reads a selection of questions aloud with a microphone and

the author responds. The problem: a lot of moving parts—the handing out of cards and writing implements, explaining the process to the audience, and then collecting the cards. At a minimum, you might find yourself buying a box of pens before every event.

Additional Q&A Tips

- Never exceed a twenty-minute Q&A session—ten to fifteen minutes is ideal.
- Avoid handing the microphone to a child or to an individual holding a notebook or loose pages in hand (this is likely the pre-ramble).
- Avoid handing the microphone to a patron with a history of rambling or confrontational questions—this is a public event, not a public forum, and you are not obligated to give everyone a voice.
- In the interest of avoiding problematic questions, encourage the author to allow library staffers to select questioners.

BOOK SIGNING

Signing books is an important component of any author event. The book signing is always an incentive for an author to agree to an event, and it can also be an incentive for your audience to attend. Because the book signing is essentially a commercial book sale, a library can take one of two perspectives: either the library is above such base transfers of wealth, leaving it to a partner (bookstore or otherwise) or the author herself; or the library can acknowledge that it should have a handle on all aspects of the event, because if any one of them goes wrong, it will reflect poorly on the library and discourage attendance at any future events.

For those firmly in the noncommercial camp, there is at least one alternative to a book sale deserving of consideration: in advance of the author appearance, purchase additional copies of the author's work(s) to put into circulation but withhold these additional copies for display just before the event, as a courtesy to event attendees. This is also a viable option when books are either particularly expensive ($40+ per copy) or when working with a smaller press that does not deal in large quantities. This strategy is also predicated on the notion that the author event takes place in the library; however, the wonders of our wireless world can allow for a laptop loaded with appropriate software (and staffed by a qualified librarian) to serve as a mobile checkout desk.

It is always advisable to add one or two copies of a presenter's book to your collection, but it is not always wise to promote this fact—at least during an event. In other words, you either sell the author's book *or* offer copies for checkout. If one of the author's goals for his library appearance is to increase book sales, do not undercut this goal by displaying five copies for checkout at a table across the hall; should a savvy patron ask the obvious question about whether the book is in the library collection, by all means answer that question.

For those with qualms about book sales, remember that the book signing is also a unique opportunity for your patrons—one that is likely to increase their affinity for the library. Book sales also promote literacy and reading—and there is never anything wrong with that. It is always wise to partner with an established bookseller. The reasons are legion: booksellers have the equipment and the experience; some have additional promotional or marketing muscle that can be applied to your event through word of mouth, a printed newsletter, or a website; and your library may have rules that restrict library staff from participating in for-profit sales. Partnering with a bookseller also takes the commercial pressure off the library—some books will not sell well or at all, and in this case a bookseller is better positioned to find another buyer for these leftover titles or even to send the books back to the publisher; furthermore, it takes the pressure off library staff to actually encourage patrons to buy. Aside from the library mentioning the book sale at the top and at the conclusion of the event, it is primarily the job of the presenting author to inspire sales, and the bookseller has a similar interest.

If you cannot partner with an established bookseller, consider the following options: simply do not conduct a book sale (which may not be an option if you have already agreed to this during your initial approach to the author); conduct the book sale yourself, making it easy by conducting only cash transactions (have change handy plus directions to the nearest ATM); or ask the author or publicist or both to conduct the book sale personally, which can certainly be awkward. Some patrons might like a previously purchased book signed, and these folks should be politely asked to wait at the end of the line—as a courtesy to the bookseller, if no one else. Those who have items other than or even in addition to books should also be asked to wait at the end of the line.

If you are expecting a sizable crowd for the book signing (any number approaching fifty), it is wise for one person to work the line with a pad of sticky notes. This person should ask those in line if there is a particular dedication that they would like the author to write; if so, this dedication should be written legibly on the sticky note by the staff member and then either given to the patron or posted on the title page of the book if it is already in hand. This saves time and the potential for confusion and misspellings when the book is given to the author.

For the sake of crowd flow, the author should have a chaperone while at the book signing table. The chaperone is there to escort any talkative or overly emotive patrons away after the signing—this can usually be done by simply reminding the patron that the line is long or that the evening has been long (thus the author needs rest or the library will soon close . . .). The author is not in a position to simply ignore or shoo such people away.

Finally, do your best to order or request an appropriate number of books to be available for sale. Estimating that one out of every ten event attendees will purchase a book is a good general rule, though a well-known author will certainly shift that equation. If you run out of books quickly, you will frustrate your audience and probably the author as well. If you order too many, the author may feel even more awkward if the grand pile of books is ignored as attendees depart.

PROMOTION

Promoting the program is certainly an important consideration, because the public is not likely to attend an event that it is unaware of. However, promotion is also one of the more mutable components of hosting an author event.

Materials

A promotional item or promotional piece can be generally defined as a print or online creation that delivers the who, what, where, and when of an event to viewers with the purpose of encouraging their attendance. Examples include printed calendars or catalogs, bookmarks, postcards, flyers, signs, outdoor banners, blast e-mails, and billboards. Some of these items might be mailed, pinned to bulletin boards, posted on your home page, or simply distributed at circulation desks. The options—at least in terms of physical dimensions—are many and can be customized to suit the particular occasion. Especially if your intent is to initiate a series of public programs, pay particular attention at the outset to designing a consistent style or format—even a brand—for these materials, much like an advertising campaign. Try to take into account any conceivable purpose to which these materials might be applied.

It is important to have a trained graphic design artist involved in this process in the early stages—and it would be helpful to have a consistent design presence. If your library hosts events infrequently—even once a month—you might make do with a graphic designer on contract, but if your library system has a graphic designer on staff then count your blessings: someone who understands not just how to make a bookmark look good but also how a printing press facility operates is a vital piece of any marketing department. Promotional pieces can easily lead to a stack of bills, but their cost overall is much less than paid advertising and can attain at least the same results—if not better.

The Media

Before approaching the media, you need to be confident of the following: your author is or is not available for media interviews (if not, just be sure not to offer an interview); you have a high-resolution (300 dpi) color photograph of the presenter available; and your author knows all the details of his local appearance. If a reporter asks something basic—such as the event start time—that stumps the author, credibility for the author and the library is lost.

The basis of all media interaction is the press release. It is preferable to send the press release approximately three weeks ahead of the scheduled event. A press release has a standard format and is intended to get the attention of the media. Sometimes a media outlet will pick up a press release and run a story based on just that. But the press release is most effective when there is a follow-up phone call to confirm that the press release has been received and to gauge interest and the likelihood of coverage.

The newspaper is the natural target for a library because newspaper readers are readers—and readers are the natural audience for a library. Do not just send your press release to a news desk or arts editor. Pay attention to the reporters who cover particular subjects (called *beats*—like "the arts beat") and the columnists for a particular newspaper section. If your event might appeal to these specialized newspaper writers, approach them with your event as a story idea and offer to schedule an interview and send a photograph of the author.

Broadcast media are much different, and the best broadcast stations to approach are noncommercial radio stations—think NPR affiliates or community/campus radio stations. Call-in talk shows that regularly interview guests are some of the best opportunities for exposure; even on the day of an event, this sort of interview can inspire listeners to attend your event. For a talk show, you will need to contact the producer (not the host) to arrange an interview. The producer is concerned about two things: whether the subject matter is interesting enough to fill a segment (be it twenty minutes or an hour) and inspire phone calls, and whether the guest is a good speaker—an author with a difficult accent or squeaky voice will probably not be booked. On the latter point, the producer might ask for an audio sample from the author.

Beyond radio talk shows, look for reporters whose previous reports or stated interests might align with your event. Radio reporters are interested in sounds—something more than just one person or a series of people talking. They like ambient sounds, sounds that provide texture or suggest a visual scene—and they love music and musicians. Radio is obviously not a visual medium. Asking a radio reporter to cover visual art is not a good approach, unless the art is incredibly easy to describe.

Television is just the opposite. Television reporters are almost exclusively interested in visuals: they like spectacle, colors, crowds, and action—or even something not seen every day. Some television reporters are interested in one-on-one interviews, but even then the reporter might express an interest in visual aids or props that the camera can focus on.

Arranging television coverage of an event is time consuming. When calling a television station, ask for the assignment desk: there are usually a few assignment desk editors on call at any time. If the editor expresses interest in your event, ask if she or he can get it on the news calendar. Always get the name of the person you talk to at the assignment desk. The primary difficulty for television is communication: there are many assignment desk editors working many different shifts, and sometimes the weekend staff is completely different. Be prepared to talk to a different editor every time you call. What interests one editor may bore another. Your press release will inevitably be lost or deleted, so be prepared to send it again. The event that you thought the previous editor had added to the news calendar may not appear on the news calendar at all.

Another difficulty is that television crews are always at the mercy of breaking news: if someone in your community is robbed an hour or two before your event, your chances of seeing the news crew go down sharply. If four news stations promise to cover your event, expect only two to actually arrive. Given patience and persistence, the camera crews will show up. Most often, a camera operator will appear solo to take footage and collect notes—maybe even to shoot a quick interview. The publicity and public awareness resulting from television coverage, however, generally justifies the difficulty in making these arrangements.

POTENTIAL PITFALLS

Imagine the flow of traffic in and out of your event space. Do not block emergency exits.

Imagine the flow of traffic outside your event space: is it obvious where attendees should park and how they should enter the venue? If not, post a greeter outside.

Always arrange chairs with aisles in mind. Do not place solid rows that are fourteen chairs in length. People generally sit on the edge of a row, preventing others from taking seats in the middle of that row. The ideal row length is five to seven chairs.

Do not design an event or series around one author or presenter before you have a commitment from that individual.

Cancellations will happen and almost always at the last minute: be prepared.

Treat the author with kindness and respect, and do all you can to ensure that you live up to your agreements as well as her expectations: authors talk to one another, and they also talk to their publicists. If you want this author—as well as her colleagues or anyone else managed by the same publicist or the same publishing company—to return to your facility, do right by her.

RESOURCES

For an example of a quality author presentation, listen to an audio recording of a presentation by Azar Nafisi at the Kansas City (Missouri) Public Library on February 25, 2009: www.kclibrary .org/event/azar-nafisi-things-i-ve-been-silent-about-0.

For an example of a quality poetry reading, listen to an audio recording of a presentation by Aimee Nezhukumatathil at the Kansas City (Missouri) Public Library on March 26, 2009: www.kclibrary.org/ event/aimee-nezhukumatathil-drive-volcano.

17

ADULT STORYTIME

David Wright

PROLOGUE

It is Monday morning at the downtown library. Patrons drop by to pick up their reserves, classes of children flock to storytime, and regulars settle in to chat, read, and ruminate. As the noon hour strikes, people gather in the auditorium, doffing raincoats, unpacking lunches or needlepoint. They are men and women, young and old, singles and couples and groups. The spiraling strains of Bernard Herrmann's soundtrack to *Vertigo* die down, the house lights dim, and the crowd settles into an expectant hush.

A librarian steps out before them and takes a seat at a small table with a microphone, clock, glass of water, and light. He opens a binder, looks out at the assembled listeners, and smiles. Peering into the semidarkness, he sees familiar faces and those of curious newcomers. He greets them, mentions a few items of library news, and then lowers his gaze to the warm light reflecting up off the pages before him. The surrounding shadows seem to deepen, the silence to sharpen. He looks up again and addresses his audience—now his conspirators—with a curious glint in his eye. "Why don't we kill somebody?" he suggests. What remains of the cares of the day drop away. They're hooked.

This scenario has unfolded at our library twice each month since that day five years ago when I first presented Thrilling Tales: A Story Time for Adults.[1] Over the years many visiting librarians have asked me about this program—what it is, how it works—and I now realize that this kind of storytime might work very well in many libraries, done many different ways. In this chapter, I'm going to tell you the story of how I started my program, discuss ways that you might produce your own adult storytime to get your creative juices flowing, and offer practical tips for selecting stories, staging the program, and reading stories—tips that I hope will save you time and trouble.

A STORYTIME FOR GROWN-UPS?

It is almost impossible to overstate how important Story is to people, and to libraries. Story is what makes us human.[2] We think in terms of narrative: it is how we make sense of our lives and our world. Hardwired for creating and interpreting stories, our dreaming minds spin tales even in our sleep. Despite the library profession's habitual (over) emphasis on Information, it is Story in its myriad forms and formats that keeps our doors open and the lights on. The readers' advisory renaissance reflects recognition of the centrality of Story to what libraries do and how the public views us, even as the Internet winnows our role as information providers.

In addition to advising readers in person and online, libraries promote and celebrate story within and beyond their walls with many different services and programs, such as book discussion groups, booktalks, and author events. Most libraries offer storytimes as well; they are one of our hallmark services. A circle of children gathered around a librarian, galvanized by unfolding events as they are elicited as if by sorcery from the pages of a book, is an image that resonates deeply with all of us. Patrons and donors who love and support libraries often owe their allegiance to those childhood visits to the library, a temple of story where high priests and priestesses unleashed the magic of reading. But storytimes are for kids, right?

Our need for story doesn't end when we turn thirteen, but abides in us from the lapsit to the nursing home. The booming audiobook industry, together with the popularity of *Selected Shorts* and similar radio and podcast narratives, shows that more and more teens and adults are tuning in to the pleasure of hearing stories read aloud. At first the idea of an adult storytime is unfamiliar, and patrons learning about my own storytime will sometimes get a quizzical look as they search for context. "Where do I get the stories? Do we read them in advance?" *No, no—it is a storytime.* "For grown-ups?" *Yes.* Then the coin drops, and—thinking of spooky stories by the campfire, or the comfort of being read to by a parent or spouse—they smile. Of course! Why on earth not!? And whether or not they decide to attend, I like to think that the library has just become that little bit more magical for them. What could be a purer and more natural expression of our vital role in preserving and promoting story than this?

MY STORYTIME: THRILLING TALES

Thrilling Tales began with a gut feeling I had when we moved into our new digs at the Seattle Public Library's landmark central branch, and I saw our 275-seat auditorium. It was a feeling common to hams everywhere, well expressed by that classic line, "Hey, kids—let's put on a show!" My instinct for keeping things simple and cheap, and my own love of reading silently and aloud, led me to the idea of a noon-hour story program that might draw seniors and also draw workers out of the surrounding buildings to come enjoy a relaxing lunch. It could be a fun drop-in program for locals and tourists who come to look at our building, offering them a taste of why we're here and what we're about.

A quick look around showed that there was a smattering of similar programs around the country and in the United Kingdom, most using literary stories. Seattle already has its own *Selected Shorts*–style series taking place just a few blocks from the library and featuring local actors reading for paying audiences. My interests and sensibilities drew me in a different direction. As a working readers' advisor who talks about books with real live flesh-and-blood readers each day, I tend to stick up for popular reading. "Never apologize for your reading tastes" is the readers' advisory motto, and the Reader's Bill of Rights is our declaration of independence from the hidebound world of literary oughts and shoulds.[3] So although there is nothing wrong with the idea per se, I wanted something that was decidedly not a "story appreciation hour" but that celebrated the sheer pleasure of Story and the delightful expectancy we experienced as children hanging on the reader's every word, wondering "what next, what next?"

Think of driving late at night on a lonely stretch of road. You tune to the AM dial and are captured by the disembodied voices from some old suspense program coming to you out of the dark. Imagine the chilling delight of gathering with friends in a dark place to share ghost stories, willing each other into a haunted state of mind. Think of how *The Twilight Zone* or *Alfred Hitchcock Presents* can so utterly draw us in with that delicious twist, even when we already know what the twist is. That is what I wanted my storytime to be: fun, captivating, a bit dangerous, and unexpected in all the expected ways.

Although I've used stories from several genres—horror, crime, fantasy, science fiction, literary fiction, and westerns—the overwhelming majority of what I read could be called suspense. Some Thrilling Tales mainstays are Roald Dahl, Shirley Jackson, Ray Bradbury, Stanley Ellin,

Patricia Highsmith, Richard Matheson, John Collier, Ruth Rendell, and Jeffery Deaver. With suspense as the guiding principle, I've featured a range of stories that includes classics and pulp fiction, contemporary surrealism and golden age ghost stories, international tales and all-but-forgotten American magazine stories. One lesser-known author whom I've used a lot is Jack Ritchie, a master of perfectly pitched, whimsical crime stories. The very first story I read was Ritchie's *A New Leaf* (aka *The Green Heart*), which begins with this great hook: "We had been married three months and I rather thought it was time to get rid of my wife."[4]

Since March 2004, I have presented Thrilling Tales on the first and third Mondays of every month, with generally between forty and eighty in attendance. For most of the program's life, I have been virtually the only person involved, selecting and reading stories, running the control booth, and doing scant marketing. Our only expense beyond my own fairly minimal time has been a single-sheet folded flyer with an annotated list of each year's stories.[5] I've had visits from local radio stations and newspapers, gracious e-mails from authors whose stories I've read, and the pure pleasure of hearing audiences snicker and sigh, murmur and gasp, indulging their love of stories and enhancing their appreciation for libraries.

YOUR ADULT STORYTIME: SOME IDEAS

Thrilling Tales is just one way of doing this program, which can be tailored to a variety of goals, communities, and venues. You'll want to present stories that interest both you and your target audience, be that a specific group or simply enough butts in the seats to make the program worthwhile. You'll need to give whatever you try plenty of time to find its audience if it is to succeed, or to fail successfully. For variety, you may wish to try out different types of storytimes; for consistency's sake, you may want to stick to one. If a regular weekly or monthly program is unrealistic given the five hundred and forty-two other things you do each day, you might opt for a seasonal or annual festival. You may find that afternoons, evenings, or weekends serve your needs, or you might extend your reach by giving multiple readings of the same story, at the library and on the road. In other words, create *your own* adult storytime. Here, in no particular order, are some ideas to help you get started.

Add a discussion. "It's the world's easiest book group!" That irresistible tagline perfectly describes the combination of a story hour and discussion group into a brilliant hybrid that may appeal to patrons for whom a traditional book group (or an additional book group) may be unfeasible. Participants can read stories in advance, or read along, or just listen. If participants prefer, stories can be read aloud round-robin style, or on a rotating basis, and story selection can also be shared. Groups can spend time working through a single author's works, read on a theme, or jump around from genre to genre. The discussion portion might also be treated as an optional part of the event, allowing a larger group to simply enjoy the story and a smaller more intimate group for discussion.[6]

Story and a movie. In an adaptation of the "book and a movie" program, participants hear a live reading of a short story and then follow up by watching the movie based on that story. Combining films and reading reaches out to a broader range of users—including men—than the traditional book group, and you'd be amazed how many films are based on surprisingly short stories.[7]

Explore cultures. Libraries seeking to include and celebrate the diversity of their communities can have a series of stories that reflect the experiences of specific cultural or ethnic groups. Culturally themed story anthologies abound.

Explore the world. You could do a story series focusing on world literature and travel writing ("Around the World in Eighty Stories"?), featuring background information on each country or region's culture and literature. Display relevant library materials, play preshow music and show slides from the place you're visiting, make note of your literary travels on a map, and provide participants with passports that they can get stamped for each fictional place they visit.

Travel through time. Highlight stories from a particular historical era (the Victorian Era, the Great Depression, the Fifties), or progress through the decades or centuries, reaching far into the distant past or tightening the focus with stories year by year. Feature supporting materials from the collection, and add context with headlines, images, and hit songs from the week the story was published.

Genres. There are myriad genres and themes to anchor a series or festival of readings, such as women's lives, men's lives, sports stories, war stories, spy stories, true crime, love stories, marriage stories, animal stories, humor, fantasy, westerns, horror, ghost stories, science fiction, myths, hardboiled mystery, parables, or true tales of adventure and survival. Focus on short-short stories, or add poetry, letters, and speeches. Just imagine the kind of crowd that might show up for a festival of vampire stories.

What's new. Explore emerging voices from hot literary journals, blogs, 'zines, and sources such as McSweeney's, Best New American Voices, or

Best American Nonrequired Reading. Try a program built on the model of the hugely popular "cringe readings" such as Mortified: Angst Written (www.getmortified.com) or Salon of Shame (http://salonofshame.com), in which participants share embarrassing passages from their old diaries, or story slams such as Moth (www.themoth.org) and Porchlight (http://porchlightsf.com).

Award winners. There are many awards for short fiction, and a series might be built around the runners-up for some of these, with a culminating event (no wagering, please!) built around the award-winning story.

Locally grown. Focus on authors from your state or region, or combine a story reading program with a writing program in your area or hosted by your library. Short stories are the lingua franca of writing programs, and having those stories read aloud, perhaps with subsequent discussion or anonymous comment cards from the audience, could be both a valuable teaching tool for the writers and an entertaining (and unpredictable!) story program for the public.

Adjust the age range. How about an all-ages storytime? Not a lapsit, but one aimed at families, with plenty of humor and suspense for all. How about an afternoon storytime focusing on teens, using stories that appeal to them (or that tie in with their schoolwork), and/or enlisting their aid to select, read, or discuss the stories? Other variations might be a mother-daughter or father-son storytime, or a storytime aimed specifically at seniors. You could aim for a particular gender, though I always think a mix is best.

Seen and heard. This is an excellent program for blind and low-vision patrons, requiring no adaptation except room for their service animals. Patrons who are hard of hearing will be glad you use amplification. This program can also be presented with a sign language interpreter to make it accessible to the hearing impaired, with added visual interest for everyone.

English as a new language (ENL). I learned what a good program this was for ENL students by accident when two local language schools started bringing classes on field trips to Thrilling Tales. Eventually I began sending a copy of the story to the teacher in advance, to be shared with the students. If you're focusing on ENL, avoid very difficult texts, or perhaps provide definitions or discuss idiomatic expressions after the reading.

Bilingual. And how about a bilingual storytime? The People and Stories/Gente y Cuentos program in New Jersey (www.peopleandstories .org) offers a terrific example of how such programs can serve a bilingual community and advance adult literacy. Reading aloud has always been a key activity in literacy learning, opening up books to new readers and bridging the distance between text and speech and between oral and literary cultures.

Add it to the mix. In addition to staging a festival of story reading, such as a week of spooky stories in October or a summer story fest held outdoors with picnics in the park or flashlights round the fire, you can add stories to other, existing programs. A story reading is a low-cost, low-fuss way to flesh out a Summer Reading Festival, a One Community One Book program, or a lecture series.

Encourage multitasking. A story reading can be the perfect accompaniment to knitting or quilting, eating lunch or drinking tea, or any other activity that doesn't distract others. How about treating a group of volunteers to a story reading while they mend books for you?[8]

Outreach. Storytimes are highly portable and can be taken to branch libraries, retirement homes, schools, hospitals, community centers, churches, prisons, factories, street corners, bars, or pretty much anywhere you need them to go.

Podcasting. This is a perfect program to include in your library's podcasts. You may want to podcast a live program or do a story program through podcasting alone.[9] As this technology entails recording (copying) and distributing (publishing) the story, you will need to address copyright concerns that are not really a factor with a simple live storytime. You can restrict your podcasts to stories and translations that you are certain are in the public domain, or get permission from the author or rights holder.[10]

A FEW PRACTICAL AND TECHNICAL TIPS

Set the stage. Very little is required here—no props or puppets, just a podium or table, a reading light, a glass of water, and some chairs. Do what you can to make the storytime space special. Lowering the lights creates a nice mood while still allowing people to knit or eat, or to gently nod off.[11] Preshow music, tailored to fit the day's story, is a wonderful, cheap way to set a mood.

Use a microphone. I strongly recommend this—in fact, I pretty much *insist* on it. Patrons who have difficulty hearing will either tell you so loudly in the middle of your story or—worse—simply stop showing up. You may be very confident in your stentorian voice, but you don't want to read like the town crier or a Broadway star, but rather in a relaxed, natural way that allows you to convey the details and nuances of the text.

I caution against using a headset mike, which doesn't respond well to the abrupt changes in volume from whispering to shouting that stories call for. An affordable stationary microphone and portable amplifier can work well for any space in or out of the library. If you're podcasting, you'll want to invest in a good digital microphone with a pop filter to soften the consonants.

"How long is this going to take?" That is a fair question. As you introduce yourself and the story, tell your listeners the reading's length and whether there will be breaks. There is no ideal length for a storytime: evening programs might last a couple of hours, while my own lunch-hour program is around forty-five minutes. I have found it works best to begin with a short-short story of five or ten minutes' duration, which warms up the audience and makes the program viable for latecomers, and then read a longer story. If you do a longer program, give people explicit permission to leave early through specified exits.

TO READ, OR NOT TO READ?

One important question that you'll want to answer right away is, who will read the stories? If you're a ham like me, the answer is obvious. If you're not, there are other ways to produce this program without doing the reading yourself. For the first year of Thrilling Tales, I made use of a resource found in most communities: theater people. Actors love to perform, and many will gladly contribute time and talent to their public library free of charge. Not everyone who would like to read stories in your library will be good at it, so you'll want to hold auditions. This is more fun than it sounds. Here's how I did mine.

I first tapped into some of the actors' networks in Seattle to get the word out about the auditions and what they were for. Most cities and towns have some sort of system for alerting actors about auditions via electronic message boards or discussion lists; just ask performers in your area. If you're in a rural system without a theater community, regular community channels will work. I called actors in groups of five for thirty-minute slots, rather than one at a time. I took a very short story and divided it into six parts, which I assigned to the actors, saving the last page for myself. I allowed the actors about ten minutes to read through the story to themselves, and then we read it aloud together, round-robin fashion, finishing with the surprise conclusion read by me. This proved much more fun than most auditions.

While the others were reading, I made notes about how well each person read and his or her particular vocal qualities: a youthful voice that might work for a child; another with a real British accent; a man's voice with the patina of experience; a woman with a low, sultry voice perfect for noir. Later, I graciously thanked those folks that I couldn't use, and I contacted the best and sent them each a small batch of stories that I thought would work well with their voice and persona. They then picked the stories they liked best, and I scheduled their readings and was there to emcee and run the show.

For the first year I alternated reading stories with several guest readers who gave some truly inspired readings. My ultimate decision to switch to reading the stories myself had less to do with my own abilities as a reader and more to do with a sense I got from some of our regular attendees that they appreciated the consistency of having a single reader rather than a variable succession of guest readers. Because it was actually less time consuming to do the readings myself, I did what most busy librarians would do and chose the easier, more sustainable path. This is not to say that having guest readers isn't a wonderful idea and a workable system, although if I *do* go back to using guest readers in the future, I will assemble a smaller company of two or three skilled readers.

HOW TO READ A STORY

Listening to a story can be hard work. If you don't believe me, try an experiment. Take a book you haven't read that has been professionally recorded, and have a friend or colleague read you the first couple of pages. Now listen to the audiobook version. You'll probably be stunned by the difference. Now, nobody is expecting you to be a professional actor or audiobook reader, but here are some small things you can do that will help your listeners and you to more fully enjoy the author's words.[12]

Rehearse. I suggest reading a story three to five times before sharing it with an audience, and *at least twice* aloud. If there's someone you can read it to, even better. You need to have a good sense of the story's structure and full command of any difficult words or grammar. The rule is, if you *think* you know how a word is pronounced, *look it up!* You'll also need to know how long the story is, and the only way to do that is by reading it aloud.

Start slowly, and don't rush. Probably the most common error for story readers is to get ahead of themselves and their listeners by reading too fast. Hearing a story takes much longer than reading it silently, so take your time and let the story unfold at its own pace. This is especially important in the establishing sequences of a story, when your listeners are just tuning in to your voice, meeting the characters, and getting their bearings in the fictional world. Even during faster-paced action sequences, heighten the intensity rather than merely upping the speed and dashing ahead of your audience.

Edit for length. If the story you're reading doesn't fit within the allotted time, you'll be tempted to rush. The best solution is to select shorter stories, but if you just love a story that is a little too long, you might do some artful editing to bring it down to size. Short stories tend not to have much fat, and it is surprisingly easy to ruin them by snipping some crucial detail or stripping them of personality to squeeze the plot in, so be *very careful* about what you cut.

Edit for content. Mine is a live program in a public library with a semi-captive audience, so I have no compunction about translating contemporary swear words into their Victorian antecedents, and I suggest you do so, too. For the same reasons, I steer clear of stories where profanity is an integral part of the style, rather than bowdlerize great gritty crime writing.

Mark up your "script." Although it may seem artificial at first, adding some notes to your photocopied story actually frees you up during a reading, allowing you to relax into the moment without getting lost or making mistakes. Develop your own notations. The following are among the things you might wish to make note of.

Emphasis. Underline key ideas, crucial information, and turning points in the plot or moments of discovery, realization, and revelation.

Character. When a story has lots of characters, I underline the different voices with colored pens to help me keep track of who is speaking. There is nothing more disconcerting than reading a line of dialogue as the crusty sea captain, only to realize halfway along that it is the little girl speaking.

Pauses and narrative breaks. Be careful about pausing too much in a story: pauses are costly and must be earned. Some are natural and necessary, so remind yourself where those are. One type of pause you do want to take occurs at places in the story where there is a change of scene or break in the narrative, such as a flashback. Mark these clearly and *use them as places to take a drink of water.*

Where to look up. Eye contact with your audience while reading a story is a tricky thing, as you don't want to get too distracted from the page itself. Marking moments of emphasis where you plan to look up can help take the pressure off, and placing your finger on them can help you quickly find your place again when you look down.

Subjective notes. Note crescendos and diminuendos in a story's pace or intensity, indicating attitude or tone. These can be literal attitudes such as "apologetic" or "smug," action cues such as "seduce" or "kill with kindness," or more affective images such as "ice cold" or "who farted?"[13]

Mark character voices. No, you don't have to be Meryl Streep or Mel Blanc to read a story. You don't have to do much, but it will be a big help to your listeners if you do a little something to help distinguish the voices of the various characters. And remember, the narrator is often a character too, even when omniscient. Often the story will give you cues as to how a particular character speaks. Here are some elements you can use, in moderation, to mark your characters' voices:

Pitch. Simply have one character talking in a higher voice, placed in your head or nose, and another speaking in a deeper chest voice.

Timbre. Vary the quality of sound, such as breathy, gravelly, nasally, and so on.

Dialect. Even if they're required by the story, you do well to keep accents very light: just a hint or a lilt. *Never read an entire story in dialect.* If every character is British or Russian, American will do just fine.

Pronunciation. Is the character precise and proper, or careless and slurred? Might she or he have some funny quirk of speech?

Pacing and manner. Again, taking your cue from the story itself, you may find some characters quick or clipped in their delivery, or deliberate and slow. Does a character have a predominant tone, such as mellifluous, gruff, chatty, taciturn, teasing, deadpan, or sardonic? Find it and use it.

Place your characters in the room. It really does help both you and your listeners to keep track of things if you read with *a physical sense* of where your speakers are in relation to each other. In two-person dialogue, think of one speaker on the left and the other on the right. In a three-person scene, add someone in the middle. Make subtle adjustments accordingly: you don't have to jump around in your chair. Try this out until it feels natural. Trust me—it helps.

Warm up. This doesn't have to be a big production, but I recommend doing some basic stretches and vocal warm-ups before a reading. Do a little yoga, hum or sing in the shower, take some deep breaths, yawn and sigh, run through a few tongue twisters, chew gum, roll your neck and shoulders. Reading aloud is all about breath and thought, so give yourself five or ten minutes to get your head in the game and get your breath relaxed and supporting you.[14]

Beware of dropping in pitch or volume at the ends of sentences. If you find you're running out of breath, you need to relax and breathe and invest in the words and the moments.

Don't comment on the story. We want to hear the story, not your opinions about it. If the story is humorous, read it straight. Let the story do the work, and do your level best to mean what you say, investing the author's, narrator's, and characters' words with sincerity and sense.

Don't worry about flubs. No matter how prepared you are, you will make mistakes while you read. Even the pros say the wrong word or lose their place in the text or lose track of which character is speaking. It is no big deal: just correct yourself and move on. So long as you don't make a fuss or get flustered about the occasional flub, your audience won't either. If you're making *lots* of flubs, prepare more.

Don't rush. Yes, I know I already mentioned this, but it is such a common problem I'm going to mention it again. *Don't rush!* This next will help.

Enjoy yourself. All your preparation is to enable you to relax, breathe, and fully enjoy sharing the story with your listeners. Find and remember the things you love about the story. Celebrate those things, and enjoy them afresh as if for the first time. This is the best job in the world. Enjoy it.

"BUT WHERE DO YOU FIND ALL YOUR STORIES?"

I get this question a lot from librarians who are curious about my storytimes, and I confess a snide impulse to reply, "You're a librarian: *look it up!*" In truth, short stories are plentiful and easy to find, but the question betrays a fact that is worth discussing here: there just aren't that many short story fans out there. In workshops, I've asked participants who would describe themselves as avid readers of short fiction to raise their hands. I have never seen more than two hands raised. I think I'd even get a bigger response if I asked for poetry buffs! The reasons for this state of affairs are varied and complex. The experience of reading short fiction is very different from that of novels. Many readers may think of short stories as highbrow aesthetic objects, unaware that most genres have an excellent short form. Brad Hooper discusses this fact in his excellent *Short Story Readers' Advisory*, a good introduction to short fiction.[15]

I confess that I was not an avid short story fan until I started doing this program. Now I can't get enough of them and am always seeking out new authors and perusing the latest story anthologies. Yes, the short story can be more demanding than the novel, with a more intense concentration of effects, which makes it, in Hooper's term, "piquant." Stories are a vivid, all-consuming experience for the reader and listener. That is what makes an adult storytime so much fun and so addictive for you and your patrons.

Some of the greatest writers of all time excelled at short stories, voices as varied as Charles Dickens, Nikolai Gogol, Anton Chekhov, Guy de Maupassant, Katherine Mansfield, Dorothy Parker, Langston Hughes, John Cheever, J. D. Salinger, Mavis Gallant, and Alice Munro. Each year scores of anthologies are published of genre and literary stories, many of them culling the best short fiction from other collections and magazines.[16] Thematic and cultural anthologies abound on topics as specific and varied as disappointed love,[17] rock and roll,[18] growing up,[19] and our multicultural society.[20] Mystery and horror alone offer thousands of collections to try.[21] In addition to current anthologies, libraries hold a rich legacy of historic collections such as *Best Detective Stories of the Year, (Saturday Evening) Post Stories,* and the several "100 Little" anthologies of short-short stories edited by Stefan Dziemianowicz and others,[22] to name just a few. You're a librarian: look them up. They're easier to find than you may think.

IN CONCLUSION

Stories are in our blood. For thousands of years, we have gathered around to hear them. As children, we came to the library for stories. Today we have "driveway moments" with NPR; even our grandparents listened with bated breath as Orson Welles convinced them that the Martians had landed, and *their* grandparents fought frenzied crowds to hear Charles Dickens read that heartrending scene with Nancy and Sykes.

Libraries are temples of story. Whatever else lies ahead for us, so long as we are to have a future, this will remain true. It is at the heart of what libraries do, not merely as repositories of data and knowledge but as centers of *meaning*. What could be a purer expression of our treasured role in preserving and promoting story than to fill the very air of our libraries with stories, for young *and* old?

NOTES

1. That opening line is from a nasty little story by Ed McBain titled "Improvisation." The story can be found in Otto Penzler's *Dangerous Women* (Mysterious Press, 2005). I read the story in December 2007, and it was later featured on NPR's *Selected Shorts*.

2. I'm hardly the only one who thinks this. See Joseph Gold, *The Story Species: Our Life-Literature Connection* (Fitzhenry and Whiteside, 2002); and Nancy Huston, *The Tale-Tellers: A Short Study of Humankind* (McArthur and Company, 2008).

3. The Reader's Bill of Rights can be found in Daniel Pennac's wonderful *The Rights of the Reader*, formerly *Better Than Life* (Walker Books, 2005), one of the best books about reading that I know of.

4. About half of Jack Ritchie's stories seem to be about husbands poisoning wives or wives poisoning husbands or both. Ritchie's stories are heavily anthologized but mostly out of print. At present you will probably need to use interlibrary loan to get the mother lode. Try *Little Boxes of Bewilderment: Suspense Comedies* (St. Martin's, 1989).

5. After the first couple of years, I decided it would be easier to select a year's worth of stories in advance. This allows me to compartmentalize the work, have a more balanced variety of tales, and produce the flyer, which turns out to be a great publicity item and one with which I've littered the surrounding office buildings. To see a list of some recent seasons, search for "Thrilling Tales" on our library blog: http://shelftalk.spl.org.

6. There seem to be a number of storytime discussions out there, including Kenton County (Kentucky) Public Library's Story Café program.

7. Examples include *The Curious Case of Benjamin Button, 2001: A Space Odyssey, The Shawshank Redemption, Field of Dreams, Minority Report, All About Eve*, and *Million Dollar Baby*. Thanks for this idea to Harlan Zinck, who does his own storytime for grown-ups with the Pierce County, Washington, library system. For ideas on other story/film pairings, take a look at Stephanie Harrison's anthology *Adaptations: From Short Story to Big Screen; 35 Great Stories That Have Inspired Great Films* (Three Rivers Press, 2005). See also Carol Emmens's *Short Stories on Film and Video* (Libraries Unlimited, 1985).

8. Thanks to Kiera Taylor, whose Fiction Allsorts program in Lake Oswego, Oregon, has combined the adult storytime with crafting and quilting circles.

9. An older version that many libraries still use is the dial-a-story, which simply broadcasts a story to callers over voice mail or an answering machine.

10. See Richard Stim, *Getting Permission: How to License and Clear Copyrighted Materials Online and Off* (Nolo, 2007).

11. Yes, this could and probably will happen at some point, but it's no problem so long as they don't snore. Think of it this way: it may be the best sleep they've had in ages.

12. For more on story reading technique, a good starting place is Robert Blumenfeld's *Acting with the Voice: The Art of Recording Books* (Limelight Editions, 2004). See also Peter Kahle's *Naked at the Podium: The Writer's Guide to Successful Readings; How to Use Drama as a Tool to Give Dynamic Readings Anywhere* (74th Street Productions, 2001).

13. Charles Dickens filled the margins of the promptbooks he used for his famed public readings with these kinds of notes, such as "Tone down to pathos" and "Terror ~ to the end!"

14. Those wanting to learn more about the care and development of the voice may profit from Cicely Berry's *Voice and the Actor* (Macmillan, 1973) and *The Actor and His Text* (Scribner, 1987), as well as Kristin Linklater's *Freeing the Natural Voice: Imagery and Art in the Practice of Voice and Language* (Nick Hern, 2006).

15. Brad Hooper, *The Short Story Readers' Advisory: A Guide to the Best* (American Library Association, 2000). There are several other reference works pertaining to short stories, including critical histories, thematic guides, and indexes.

16. *Best American Short Stories* (Houghton Mifflin, 1978–), *Best American Mystery Stories* (Houghton Mifflin, 1997–), *Year's Best Fantasy and Horror* (St. Martin's Press, 1990–), *The O. Henry Prize Stories* (Doubleday, 1919–2002; Anchor Books, 2003–), *Best New American Voices* (Harcourt, 2000–).

17. In fact there were *two* such anthologies one year: Meredith Broussard's *Dictionary of Failed Relationships: 26 Tales of Love Gone Wrong* (Three Rivers Press, 2003) and B. Delores Max's *Dumped: An Anthology* (Grove Press, 2003).

18. Greg Kihn, *Carved in Rock: Short Stories by Musicians* (Thunder's Mouth Press, 2003).

19. Paula Deitz, *Writes of Passage: Coming-of-Age Stories and Memoirs from the Hudson Review* (Ivan R. Dee, 2008), among others.

20. Stacy Bierlein, *A Stranger among Us: Stories of Cross Cultural Collision and Connection* (OV Books, 2007); and Chandra Prasad, *Mixed: An Anthology of Short Fiction on the Multiracial Experience* (W. W. Norton, 2006).

21. If you think you hate horror stories, try two of my favorite anthologies of subtle horror: Joan Kessler's *Night Shadows: Twentieth-Century Stories of the Uncanny* (David R. Godine, 2001), and Michele Slung's *Stranger: Dark Tales of Eerie Encounters* (Harper Perennial, 2002). Mystery skeptics may be pleasantly surprised by Michele Slung's *Murder and Other Acts of Literature: Twenty-four Unforgettable and Chilling Stories by Some of the World's Best-Loved, Most Celebrated Writers* (St. Martin's Press, 1997); and Otto Penzler's *Vicious Circle: Mystery and Crime Stories by Members of the Algonquin Round Table* (Pegasus, 2007). If you find yourself daunted by the sheer volume of crime anthologies, you can start right at the top with Tony Hillerman's *Best American Mystery Stories of the Century* (Mariner, 2001); Linda Landrigan's *Alfred Hitchcock's Mystery Magazine Presents Fifty Years of Crime and Suspense* (Pegasus, 2006); and Jeffery Deaver's *A Century of Great Suspense Stories* (Berkley Prime Crime, 2001).

22. *Best Detective Stories of the Year* (E. P. Dutton, 1945–1981); *Post Stories* (Little, Brown, 1935–1941; Random House, 1945–1962); e.g., Stefan Dziemianowicz, Robert Weinberg, and Martin Harry Greenberg, eds., *100 Tiny Tales of Terror* (Barnes and Noble, 1996).

Part 5

Expanding Readers' Advisory Services

18

READERS' ADVISORY BY PROXY FOR TEENS

Heather Booth

Some readers' advisory requests strike fear in the heart of even the most stalwart young adult librarian: "*Holes* is the only book I've ever read and I want something *exactly like it*." Or, "I need a book for a report that deals with a historical event between 1890 and 1912, and it needs to have pictures, but it has to be short because the report is due tomorrow." Or, "I want to read a book like *Speak*, but funny." As long as the request is coming from the young patron who hopes to read the book, you can usually find something that will match the patron's needs by carefully conducting a readers' advisory interview and by using all of the resources for matching teens and books that you have at your disposal. For many librarians though, the most difficult book requests come not from teen readers, but from their parents, teachers, or adult friends: "I need a book for my son. Where are your books for high school freshmen?" Or, "My daughter doesn't read, but I want a book that will get her to like reading." Or, "He only reads junk. Can you recommend some quality literature?" On the surface, these requests seem simple enough. Plenty of books are interesting and readable for fourteen-year-old boys, are excellent for reluctant readers, or are literary greats. So what's the problem?

Helping parents select books for their teens, or readers' advisory by proxy, is an endeavor fraught with unique issues. Does the parent know what books the teen has already read, and—more important—enjoyed? Are you expected to find books that primarily meet the parent's approval or the teen's interest? Will the parent be willing to take a selection of books back to the teen, or is the one book you select going to be the teen's only reading choice? When helping parents find books for their teens, librarians' standard operating procedures for readers' advisory go awry because it is

Reprinted from *Young Adult Library Services* 5, no. 1 (Fall 2006).

often unclear who the patron really is. Is it the parent who is looking for the material, or is it a teen whose reading interests are unfamiliar to you?

When parents come to the library seeking books for their teens, even if they have very little information on which to base a recommendation, and even if they have a very firm idea of what their teen *should* read, we need to remember that it is a good thing that the parents are actively attempting to seek out reading material for their child. Parents are allies in connecting teens with books, and readers' advisory by proxy should be approached as a bridge-building activity, not a chore. Many teenagers are astoundingly busy, and sometimes the only way for a young person to have a connection to books is for parents to bring them into the house. When parents insist on a specific type of book—a classic, or something with which they are familiar—they are not *necessarily* trying to censor or control their child's reading material. It is quite possible that what they seek is a shared reading experience. A book that both parent and child have read can be a way for parents to connect to their quickly and drastically changing adolescent. It is equally possible that some parents aren't even aware that librarians can and do provide reading suggestions, and simply ask for titles familiar to them because they don't know where to find suggestions. Assure these parents that you are glad to help get some great books into the hands of their teens, that you are glad they are involved in making books readily available to their children, and that you are happy to provide suggestions for whatever type of reading their teens would like.

This is not to say that the interaction will always be an easy one. Parents aren't always aware of their teens' reading interests. For example, a parent may know that his teen used to like reading high fantasy, but may be unaware that she has been on a manga kick for the past three months. Additionally, even if the parent is up on his child's reading interests, it is a rare parent who can remember which books that teen has read or which he didn't care for. Even if the teen has relayed information about the type of books to bring home, librarians still must play a delicate game of telephone. Maybe the teen read *Jurassic Park* and told his mom he didn't like the dinosaur aspect, but since the teen is not around, you don't know if books with dragons or man-eating alligators would be suitable. After you determine as best you can what the teen would like to read based on the parent's comments, you are still challenged by not knowing the teen's reaction to the books. Unlike working directly with a teen at the library—who can page through the books you select, choose or reject titles, and allow you to make a few more suggestions—you rarely get a second round during a single visit from a parent selecting books.

So what is the remedy for these issues? Begin by getting to the root of the request through solid reference interview techniques. Determine if the request is intended to fill an assignment, is a teen's request, or stems from the parent's interest in finding a book for the teen. This should help to direct the focus of the suggestions. To receive an indication of what type of material may work best, try asking if the parent recalls the last book the teen read and whether or not the teen commented on the book. Inquiring about the types of movies or television shows the teen enjoys could also indicate which genres may be more appealing. If the parent doesn't remember or doesn't know, ask if the teen is accessible by phone. If the teen is at home or available to take a call on a cell phone, a few quick questions may help to ensure that the teen will be open to reading the books you send home. You need not operate in an isolated bubble if the information you need to provide excellent service, instead of adequate service, is readily available. Additionally, this demonstrates to the teen that you are sincerely interested in selecting books that he or she *wants* to read, and that the selection of books that winds up at home isn't the result of a great librarian-parent conspiracy!

Consider devising more creative methods of conveying information to your teen patrons who are just too busy to come in. But even if an over-booked schedule isn't the primary reason why parents are at the library instead of teens, extending some of these services will help to convey to teens that the library is a place that is welcoming and interested in serving them. Sending prepared booklists to go along with the books, offering a departmental e-mail address for follow-up and further suggestions, or even providing information about your library's website, online catalog, or virtual reference services are ways to make the library accessible to teens. If it is clear that the parent is really the one seeking the information, assure him or her that you truly do want to know how the teen likes the books you have suggested, and that during the next visit to the library, you would like the chance to suggest a few more titles, whether the teen liked the books or not. Feedback on recommendations by proxy can help you hone your skills at finding books appropriate for the intended reader.

The reality of modern teen life means that many of our readers' advisory interactions for teens will actually take place through their parents. If we are prepared for the slightly different mechanisms by which we must conduct the readers' advisory interview in these circumstances, and strive to extend our services beyond the face-to-face interactions we ultimately desire, the teens in our communities will know that the library is *their* library, too.

19

READERS' ADVISORY FOR OLDER ADULTS

Alicia Ahlvers

Working with older adults can be one of the most rewarding patron inter-actions in the library. Apart from the preschool crowd, no other group is as openly appreciative when they receive the help they need. The elder demographic is often the most loyal group of library supporters and the most likely to form long-term attachments to a favorite librarian or staff person.

One reason older adults are often so appreciative when receiving good or excellent customer service is that in today's fast-paced world, ser-vice staff often can be impatient with those who need extra attention, and therefore good service will stand out as extraordinary. Because seniors fre-quently need extra assistance due to physical problems, the lack of extra time and attention can be particularly disheartening for bright, aware, older adults already mourning the loss of vision or hearing. It is important for librarians working with seniors to remember that becoming an older adult can be challenging and stressful. We all know people who embrace the changes that come with aging, but for many the loss of mobility and independence can be frightening.

Try to keep in mind that, as do all humans, some older adults crave human contact and may only get this contact from their library encoun-ters, especially as longer life spans and far-flung families mean more and more older adults are cut off from their support systems. Look at this as a patron need and understand that library staff may have to spend more time working with older adults in order to help them find library materi-als. A few extra minutes with a librarian may enrich a patron's life, not only by gathering information to provide well-thought-out readers' advi-sory but also by giving the gift of time. After all, studies show that older adults thrive if they have at least three regular contacts with whom to converse. For those of us who entered the world of librarianship to make a difference, becoming one of these important contacts is a special gift.

When working with older adults, it can be useful to know something about the different generations. The three distinct categories used to refer to older adults include the G.I. Generation, the Silent Generation, and the baby boomers, who are just now starting to retire.

THE G.I. GENERATION

The G.I. Generation (GIs) was born between the years 1900 and 1922. This generation tends toward civic duty and fiscal responsibility, and they are big believers in agreement and conformity. As a group they believe in working together to achieve the best for everyone. They stay busy in retirement or don't retire at all and dislike people they perceive to be wimps or slackers. Because this group believes that the harder they work, the more they are rewarded, they often have a strong sense of entitlement.

These traits mean that a person from this generation is not afraid to speak his or her mind. This group will let you know in great detail if your book recommendation is on target. They often have strong feelings early on about a novel, and they are willing to tell you when a book has missed the mark. Luckily, they often have a strong gallant streak to temper their criticisms and usually are willing to give you several chances to get it right.

The GIs are particularly fond of sentimental stories and novels with characters from their generation. In addition, they often are guided by best-seller lists, newspaper recommendations, or any other books "everybody is reading" or should have read. Classic novels that they "should" read and recommendations by loved ones also fall into this category. Remember, conformity is a characteristic of this group.

The GIs have a rather black-and-white outlook, a strong patriotic viewpoint, and a deep interest in politics. If a novel reflects this world outlook, they usually like it. A strong dislike for profanity in novels is also an important consideration. Christian mystery, romance, and fiction and cozy mystery large print imprints are very useful when selecting for this type of customer, even when she or he is not interested in the Christian theme.

Also look for cozy mysteries that are in high demand. Authors such as Lilian Jackson Braun, Mary Higgins Clark, and Alexander McCall Smith are current favorites. For the same reasons that make cozy mysteries popular, Christian mysteries and romance are also in high demand. Patrons report that these books are comforting reads and are assured that there will not be any unpleasant or unwanted surprises while reading these novels. Romantic suspense and contemporary romance are on the upswing with the older adult crowd. Exciting plot lines make these subgenres popular. Some of these titles have some of the same elements as the cozy mysteries, but many can be quite explicit, so it pays to know your authors. For example, Nora Roberts, the queen of romantic suspense, can be a little racy for some customers, while others love her.

The lack of useful subject headings for romance and, to a lesser extent, mysteries can make these genres difficult to search. Books aren't often assigned sensuality ratings or subgenre notes, and these elements can be of vital importance to many readers. The readers' advisor can keep up in these areas by reading extensively in the romance and mystery genres, using reviews, participating in fan electronic discussion lists, and keeping an eye on the genre websites in order to assess the profanity level and sex scenes. A useful website for romance, www.likesbooks.com, includes "heat level" ratings from "kisses" to "burning." When you're not familiar with an author, it is useful to check the reviews to see how his or her books are typically ranked.

The following are the G.I. Generation's most frequently requested authors:

Maeve Binchy	Rosamunde Pilcher
Jimmy Carter	Belva Plain
Zane Grey	LaVyrle Spencer
Jan Karon	Margaret Truman
Louis L'Amour	Phyllis Whitney

THE SILENT GENERATION

The Silent Generation covers seniors who were born between 1923 and 1942. This generation believes in working hard and paying your dues. They like security and stability, dislike debt, believe in clean living, and are often quite reserved. The Silent Generation has a strong stoic streak and doesn't want to be a bother. This attitude can present problems when attempting to provide readers' advisory assistance. You will have to ask people from this group to let you know if they don't like a book you recommend. You may also have to repeatedly reassure these customers that reserving extra books or spending additional time isn't a bother and that they are not intruding when they call or visit the library.

In terms of readers' advisory, the Silent Generation is very willing to accept the advice and recommendations of experts. They will try books recommended by celebrities, newspapers, educators, and librarians, and they have a great deal of faith in the experts. Members of this generation remain interested in connecting with the younger generations and are willing to explore work by new authors. On the other hand, they also like novels that show empowered older adults leading full and interesting lives. Authors Haywood Smith, Joan Medlicott, and Alexander McCall Smith are popular for this reason.

Some individuals from this generation also develop an interest in inspirational and spiritual matters and will ask for authors who explore these issues in a broader context. Caroline Myss, John Edward, and Sylvia Browne are possible favorites.

Frequently requested authors for the Silent Generation include the following:

Barbara Taylor Bradford	Tim LaHaye
Sandra Brown	Fern Michaels
Patricia Cornwell	Walter Mosley
Catherine Coulter	Robert B. Parker
Janet Dailey	James Patterson

BABY BOOMERS

When the baby boomers (1943–1963) start to retire, watch out. All the traditional ideas about older adults will go out the window. The motto of this group could be "If you've got it, flaunt it," and their key characteristics may include a tendency to be talkative, bossy, inquisitive, and competitive. Boomers also see themselves as trend makers instead of trend followers. In contrast to the preceding generations, they do not take the idea of aging philosophically and are more likely to deeply resent being referred to as senior citizens or elderly. Boomers are not afraid of debt and they like to spend money, so count on them having all of the latest gadgets and toys. Those who become homebound are more likely to be willing and able to use the online catalog to reserve or download books. They will also appreciate this technology because they are used to having immediate service. They expect to have the book in their hands as soon as they ask for it. Downloadable books and audiobooks will likely become very popular with this generation.

The G.I. and Silent Generations tend to prefer the mystery and romance genres, and few in these age groups will express interest in other genres. Boomers, on the other hand, will use all the traditional sources for obtaining book suggestions, and online book sites are popular selection tools. Fans of certain genres will seek out romance, mystery, or science fiction electronic discussion groups and will expect to walk into the library and find the newest titles waiting on the shelf. Boomers will accept more sex, violence, and profanity, so interest in true crime and horror stories will increase. They will be much more particular about getting just the right book. They look for riveting tell-all books, fast-paced thrillers, and conspiracy mysteries, which helps explain why *The Da Vinci Code* by Dan Brown became such a huge hit.

Although the Silent Generation will likely be patient with the trial-and-error process of readers' advisory, boomers will be much less willing to spend months working with you to fine-tune your recommendations. You will have only a few chances to get it right, and then they will move on. On the other hand, they will be willing to try less well-known authors and "sell" them to their family and friends if they like them. And once you have sold them on the new library conveniences and earned their trust, they will become loyal library users.

Boomers' most frequently requested authors are these:

David Baldacci	Dean Koontz
Suzanne Brockmann	Terry McMillan
Janet Evanovich	Richard North Patterson
Jonathan Kellerman	Anne Rice
Stephen King	Nora Roberts

The following authors are extremely popular with all generations:

Lilian Jackson Braun	Sue Grafton
Mary Higgins Clark	John Grisham

INTRA-GENERATIONAL CATEGORIES

Two additional categories can have a profound effect on the different generations. These categories can be referred to as the *young-old* and the *old-old*. The major difference between the two groups is that regardless of age the young-old are healthy and the old-old are not. The young-old are energetic, vibrant, and active. The old-old suffer loss of mobility, are often in pain, suffer increased hearing and vision loss, and do not have opportunities to interact with others, especially those outside their age group. This group craves interaction with children and younger generations and values social interaction a great deal.

THE READERS' ADVISORY INTERVIEW

Step One: Determine Genre Preferences

If you have the time and the customer is willing, an excellent way to begin is to have her fill out a questionnaire about her reading preferences. After she completes the questionnaire, you can ask her for more detailed information. If you and the patron do not have the time to fill out a survey, simply ask what types of materials she prefers.

If a patron is primarily interested in nonfiction, especially if she has specialized interests, the level of subject detail in the MARC records makes titles fairly easy to locate. Some patrons already have lists of authors and titles of books that they are interested in and will come to the library to request them as needed. Encourage these patrons to reserve books ahead of time to ensure that the volumes they want are available, especially if browsing the shelves is difficult for them. If they have Internet access from their home, teach them how to reserve titles using the library's online catalog. If they don't have access to the Internet, another option is to send them home with vendor catalogs or review journals. Please make sure the catalogs are from companies your library actually uses to order materials. Patrons can browse the catalog or journal, call in an order, and have it ready to go when they get to the branch. If print size in the catalog is an issue, see if your state library or other agencies in your community have small magnifying glasses to give away as promotional material.

The most challenging patrons are those who would like you to select their ten large print mysteries or twenty spoken-word romances a month. Of course, the first question is, "What kinds of books do you like to read?" Some patrons will have detailed information about types of books, specific authors, and favorite titles or subjects. Others have not given this question much thought and can only hint at broad outlines of their preferences. In this case, you might want to ask what type of television programs they prefer, what hobbies they have, and what current events they find interesting. With these questions, you and the patron can come up with one or two genres or a couple of subjects. Because those of us in the readers' advisory game know how many different subgenres exist, this information can be a jumping-off point for gathering information in the readers' advisory interview. Keep in mind that sometimes these genre requests are deceptive. A patron may ask for paperback romances set in the South or West, but after working with her for a while, it may become clear that what she really wants is a western.

Try to keep the trends and characteristics of each generation in the back of your mind, but always remember to treat every older adult as an individual. When asked what she liked to read about, 93-year-old Sadie stated that she wanted "sex, sex, sex," to the surprise and delight of the librarian working with her. Although it is important to be aware of the generational trends discussed earlier, it is equally important to remember that each individual has a type of book that speaks to him or her in a personal way. Books about ladies living in small towns may be a current trend, but don't jump in with a suggestion too quickly. Wait until you have conducted the full readers' advisory interview before suggesting titles.

Another challenge to working with older readers may occur when a middle-aged adult comes in to pick out books for a parent. A daughter may have an image of what she thinks her sweet 80-year-old mother should be reading, but really have no idea what books actually bring her mother delight. In these situations, it may be useful to call the parent or have the older adult call you to provide more information about reading tastes. This method could be difficult if the older adult has hearing problems, in which case a questionnaire could be sent home asking for more detailed information.

Step Two: Determine Format Preferences

It is important in readers' advisory interactions with older patrons to note a hearing or vision disability because recommending a list of books and then not being able to find them in the necessary format is frustrating for both you and your patron. After taking a reader's personal information, an important question to ask is the preferred reading format. Ask patrons to rank their format choices. Luckily in today's world, there are a variety of format options from which to choose. Many publishers often offer simultaneous release of best sellers in all formats as a selling point.

Multiple formats suited to older adults or anyone with a physical disability are available in today's library market. These include large print books (16-point print is the standard) in hardcover and paperback, books on tape, books on compact discs, MP3s on compact discs, downloadable books, and spoken-word books. Tomorrow there will be options we haven't even dreamed of yet.

Many older adults can still read regular print, but for others such print is difficult to see clearly. Large print books are a great option for anyone experiencing loss of vision. Imagine trying to read an entire novel printed in very small type. It would be frustrating and tiring and would become a chore rather than a pleasure. Several mainstream publishers deal with large print, and each has its own specialty and mission. Be sure your library has access to a nice variety of these titles.

Downloadable books are predicted to become the wave of the future for those needing large print, but we aren't there yet. Access to downloadable spoken-word books may cause problems. Many older adults live on fixed incomes and may not be able to afford the latest technology, while others may be unwilling to learn or fearful about technology. However, older adults are beginning to jump on the technology bandwagon as they discover the joy of e-mail with their grandchildren. Limited selection, lack of superior-quality readers at an affordable price, and fear of technology make this format difficult to recommend at present, but look out as the baby boomers start to retire.

Spoken-word cassettes and CDs have similar problems of availability, although producers are striving to improve title selection and simultaneous release dates. In addition to availability issues, spoken-word books often have other issues that are frequently mentioned by listeners with hearing loss: the narrator reads too fast, the narrator's accent makes hearing each word difficult, and higher-pitched or softer-spoken voices are difficult to hear. If you have a large population of older adults visiting your library, it is worth your time to find narrators who have slow, clear diction. Of course, their reading must also be lively and interesting.

Another option for small libraries with very limited selection or for patrons who are not particularly mobile is to use your state library's Talking Book program. Although the quality of the recordings is not comparable to that produced by publishing houses, this program features more variety. In addition, the special player, the four-track cassettes, and the postage are free to eligible candidates. Talking Book programs are available to anyone who is visually impaired or physically unable to hold and read a book. Obtain application forms from your state library and keep them on hand for patrons.

In addition to vision problems, older readers may have arthritis or diminished physical strength. These patrons may have trouble holding or carrying hardcover and other heavy books. Some older patrons have difficulty holding books for long periods, so you may have to mine the very limited supply of paperback versions of large print titles. In a best-case scenario, older patrons with physical disabilities will not have vision problems and can find an endless supply of paperbacks. In more extreme cases, however, you might have to help them adapt to using the spoken-word format.

Step Three: Determine Style Preferences

Once genre and format preferences have been established, ask the patron to talk about a recent book he has read. This step can give a lot of information about the style of book that a patron wants, although you may find that some patrons have difficulty verbalizing their preferences or even describing the book. If this is the case, ask the patron if he likes a fast-paced book with lots of plot twists or a descriptive story about relationships. This choice will usually give him a starting point for describing the book in more detail. Sometimes you may have to read or skim the book the patron has just described in order to become familiar with its elements and understand what appeals to the reader.

Step Four: Make Recommendations and Follow Up

Once you have gathered enough information, you can make recommendations, but this is not the end of the interaction. It is important to stress to your patron that this is just a starting point and that having honest feedback will help you make even better recommendations in the future. This is particularly important with members of the Silent Generation, who will not want to criticize your recommendations or take up your time. Also, if you find that your interactions with patrons are frequently rushed or interrupted, it can be helpful to let patrons know times when they can call or find you at the service desk, or when the library is less busy. In this way, readers' advisory interviews can be unhurried and productive, and patrons won't feel pressured or guilty about taking up your time.

OVERCOMING BARRIERS

Physical disabilities, lack of reliable transportation, and different world-views or perspectives can all create barriers to a successful readers' advisory interview. Librarians need to be particularly sensitive to any patron who has a hearing or vision loss. Because older adults often have these problems, it is important to watch for warning signs.

When suggesting titles, ask how often the patron is able to come to the library. Also ask how many books she will need until her next library visit. Sometimes an older adult won't get as many books as she would like because she can't carry the books to her car or other transportation. This may also be a reason why patrons stick with tried-and-true authors: they can count on having something to read before the next library visit. If you have the time or if another staff person is available, you may want to offer to carry these patrons' books to the car.

If your senior readers are depending on rides from family members, friends, or care providers, they may also be anxious about incurring overdue charges or having their library card taken away. Let them know about library policies for telephone renewal and overdue fines. Also, point out any special services you offer, such as home delivery service or books-by-mail. A special "fine-free day for seniors" each month may offer financial relief for those who have transportation issues. If your library does not currently offer these services, you may wish to consider adding them. If these are not options, you may be able to offer extended checkout or create special library cards that have extended checkout or a no-fine feature. Vision problems may make it difficult to know when the books are due. Be sure to offer to use large print for the date stamp or the printed receipt, and have large print versions of booklists or other promotional material on hand.

If you are interested in adding a books-by-mail program to your service plan, your library can create a fairly simple and inexpensive program. A Friends group is a good resource for funding to purchase canvas mailers. Grants are also available to fund these types of programs, and durable mailers can be obtained for very little money. Manila envelopes are a low-cost alternative, although they are not as sturdy as the canvas mailers. Postage is usually the biggest expense in a books-by-mail program. Under the U.S. Code, title 39, sections 3403–3405, libraries may be able to mail items to qualifying recipients free of charge. There are very clear regulations about patron eligibility, the wording of mailing labels, and the types of material that can be included. This option can be helpful when mailing large print or spoken-word materials to people of any age who have visual impairments. Most libraries require patrons to fill out an application for the service (with a doctor's signature) to weed out those not qualified and to verify that a patron is visually disabled in case questions arise.

All these suggestions are designed to make the readers' advisory experience more pleasurable for you and the older reader. Every community is unique and has its own set of challenges, so take a look at your older adult users and see how closely they match up to generational characteristics. Then tailor the ideas in this chapter to fit your community. Above all, enjoy your older adults. They will reward you with their enthusiasm, loyalty, and gratitude. Who knows, you may even make a new friend with stories to tell and knowledge to share.

Sample Application for Homebound Services

Please take just a minute to fill out the following application. It is our goal to serve anyone in the Kansas City Public Library District who is homebound and unable to reach a library due to physical disability.

Name _____

Address _____

City _____ State _____ Zip _____

Phone _____ Birthdate _____

How did you hear about us? _____

_____

_____

If you have a Kansas City Public Library card please write the number here:

_____

I understand that Home Bound Books is a service offered to those with a physical disability that prohibits their visiting the local library. I certify that I am eligible for this service under those conditions.

Signature _____ Date _____

Health care professional _____

Format preferences (please circle all that apply)

Large Print   Regular Print   Paperback   Hardback   Audio Cassette

Please tell us what you like to read (circle all that apply)

Romance   Mystery   Suspense   Western   Nonfiction   Travel   Historical

Biography   Other _____

Favorite authors or subject preferences _____

_____

_____

_____

_____

(cont.)

Sample Application for Homebound Services (cont.)

What is your favorite book and what did you like best about it? _____

_____

_____

_____

_____

Other notes _____

_____

_____

_____

_____

Thank you for your interest in the Home Bound Books program. Please fill out this form as completely as possible, sign it, and mail it back to us. We will contact you as soon as we have had time to process your application.

20

READERS' ADVISORY
FOR INCARCERATED POPULATIONS

Kate Pickett and CJ Sullivan

Working with readers who are incarcerated is a unique experience for any librarian. In many facilities, regardless of security level, the only item allowed in a resident's cell or room is a paperback book. In a place where clothes, food, and daily activities are decided for the residents by others, the choice of what book to read is one of the few decisions they get to make for themselves. It is a powerful and possibly nerve-racking responsibility to help readers who are incarcerated find their reading material. However daunting this task might seem, your goals are the same as those for a traditional readers' advisory interaction: find the right book for the right reader.

THE PEOPLE

The first step to a good interaction with an incarcerated reader is to have a good relationship with the administration at the facility. If you are working in the facility, the administrator might be your manager, or if your library is offering outreach services to the facility, this person might be the volunteer coordinator. Administrative support is essential before you can move forward with readers' advisory. If members of the administration agree that reading is a positive activity for the residents, they will work with you to help make reading materials accessible and will be valuable allies in the case of a challenge.

Second, develop a relationship with staff and teachers in the facility. Talk with them about their own favorite books. Staff interacts with residents daily; if a staff member or teacher is well respected among residents, his or her recommendations will be popular choices.

Last, you need to have buy-in from the residents themselves. Help them understand that reading is not an academic activity by suggesting titles with which they can really connect. This facility may be the only place where residents have the time or the attention to sit down and read a book cover to cover. You can help them find the book that will make them want to read when they are no longer residents of the facility. But remember, the books you want to connect residents with are the ones *they* want to read, not the ones you—or the administrators at the facility—want them to read. No matter how much you want them to read inspirational stories about characters in similar situations, those may not interest them. Instead, just help these readers find a book they would love to read.

THE FACILITY

There are several types of facilities where you may come in contact with readers who are incarcerated. We will briefly describe the two types of facilities with which we have experience—residential centers and detention centers—and the programs that we provide there.

Residential centers are often focused on helping residents with abuse problems (physical or substance). Residents may stay for six months or more, which helps in developing relationships with readers for more successful and meaningful interactions. Residential facilities have more relaxed guidelines and staff, which encourage more flexible relationships with their residents and allow inhabitants to have more access to information. Two currently existing programs are Stories about Women (SAW) and Stories about Men (SAM), weekly short story and book discussion groups cofacilitated by a librarian and a corrections staff member that meet for one hour at the adult residential facility. Copies of the readings are provided in advance to the director of the center, a practice that helps to foster a healthy relationship with administration. Women are required to attend for their first three months at the center; men, from the six-month intensive drug/alcohol rehabilitation program, participate on a voluntary basis. We make efforts to find books and short stories that will facilitate discussion and be relevant to their lives. At the end of each session, participants are encouraged to talk about what they are reading or a favorite title they could recommend to the group.

Detention centers can serve a variety of needs and can differ drastically in the amount of time residents spend there (from overnight stays to sentences of many years). This variation makes it more difficult to provide quality readers' advisory interactions. It's quite possible you may see a resident only once; thus, every interaction must be the most positive experience for the inhabitant that the library staffer can manage. These facilities also tend to be more rigid than residential centers, controlling more of the residents' lives and limiting the information residents may have access to and how they can access it. This increases the possibility of readers' service providers encountering censorship. One program that we offer to the local juvenile detention center is Read to Succeed. Librarians act as facilitators for short-story discussion groups, and after discussion has ended, residents may choose from a selection of books compiled by librarians and donated by the Friends of the Library. Limiting the selection makes it necessary for librarians to find books that have broad appeal and represent all points of view.

SELECTION RESTRICTIONS

Three qualities are important to note in a book for a reader who is incarcerated: quality, relevance, and reading level. Although the collection for use in the detention facility may be limited due to lack of funds or restrictions set by the administration, it is important to look for these factors in all the books you recommend.

Strive to fulfill any readers' advisory requests as quickly as possible to encourage the residents to continue reading, but also remember that the quality of the book is important. Quality is defined both as the literary merit of the writing and as the ability of the book to fill the reader's need. This is when knowledge of the collection and popular literature is essential. When it is not possible to fill a readers' advisory request with the right book, reconnect with the reader to make other suggestions.

Find books that are relevant to residents' lives and the world as it is now. This is especially true of nonfiction, and although it may be difficult if the facility has a small or aged collection from which to choose, trying to find the newest materials is always appreciated by residents. If the library or facility has the funds to put a brand-new book in a resident's hands, do it. Detention center inhabitants do not often get to handle something that has not been used by someone else, and cracking open a new book selected just for them may make the reading experience a little more significant.

Reading level is also important to consider when working with readers who are incarcerated. Some residents read below their age level, and this gap may be especially obvious in a juvenile facility with residents as young as 9 or 10. Select books that have high appeal but a very approachable reading level. Choose more than one book for a resident, and help potential readers find books that match their reading skills. Residents of a detention center or residential facility may be hesitant to admit difficulty with reading in front of other residents or staff. Be open and approachable to residents in these situations. Be aware of body language and other nonverbal behaviors that may help you estimate reading ability. It is always better to give out a book that is below a resident's reading level (but not interest level) and have the reader state it was too easy than to give out one that is too challenging. Remember, leisure reading is not supposed to be a struggle.

THE BOOKS

Find out what types of books are allowed in the facility. Be aware that it is common for detention centers to allow only paperback books in the cells. This practice can be frustrating for residents who want the most recent best sellers, but it also creates a good opportunity to promote those best-seller read-alike lists for the books they can't yet get in the facility. Talk to members of the administration and find out if any genres or topics are off-limits (frequently censored topics include erotica, homosexuality, gangs, and drug abuse).

Ask residents, staff, and teachers what they are reading. Because residents at a detention center or residential facility have limited access to information, they have limited ways to find out about new reading materials. Like other readers, residents will turn to their neighbors for suggestions. Find out who or what the reading trendsetters are suggesting and familiarize yourself with the material. Knowing authors or series that are similar will come in handy when ten readers ask you for the same book that was recommended by a respected staff member or resident.

Weeding is another great way to see which titles or authors are popular with residents. Look for books that are particularly beaten up or obviously well read. Note these titles and authors and try to find new copies. Unless a book is completely falling apart, do your best to keep a popular title until replacement copies are available. These are the titles that should be on your own To Read pile for creation of future read-alike lists.

Try to keep an open mind when working with readers who are incarcerated. Just like in the world outside detention facilities, each reader is seeking something different from a book. Some want escapist fantasy, some want suspenseful mysteries, and some want true tales about people they know or can empathize with. It can be easy to stereotype "detention center reads" as books about religion, drugs, gangs, violence, and murder.

However, best sellers and memoirs are just as popular with the readers with whom we have worked as are any of these genres. Here are some authors and titles that have had perennial appeal.

Memoirs and Nonfiction

Barbara Ehrenreich (*Nickel and Dimed*)
James Frey (*A Million Little Pieces*)
Jack Gantos (*Hole in My Life*)
Jon Krakauer (*Into the Wild*)
Anne Morrow Lindbergh (*Gift from the Sea*)
The Autobiography of Malcolm X
Dave Pelzer (*A Child Called "It"*)
Mary Roach (*Stiff*)
Tupac Shakur (*The Rose That Grew from Concrete*)
Hunter S. Thompson (*Fear and Loathing in Las Vegas*)
Jeannette Walls (*The Glass Castle*)
Frank Warren (*PostSecret*)

Mystery/Suspense

Dan Brown
Michael Crichton
Gail Giles
Lisa Jackson

Stephen King
James Patterson
Karin Slaughter
Stuart Woods

Fantasy/Science Fiction

Ray Bradbury
Charlaine Harris (*Dead until Dark*)
Cormac McCarthy (*The Road*)

Stephenie Meyer (*Twilight*)
Philip Pullman (*The Golden Compass*)

Street Lit/Drugs

Anonymous (*Go Ask Alice*)
Bluford series
Coe Booth (*Tyrell*)

Ellen Hopkins (*Crank*)
Sister Souljah

Fiction

Laurie Halse Anderson (*Speak*)

Elizabeth Berg

Maeve Binchy

Leif Enger (*Peace like a River*)

Janet Evanovich

John Grisham

S. E. Hinton (*The Outsiders*)

Sue Monk Kidd (*The Secret Life of Bees*)

Walter Dean Myers (*Monster*)

Patricia McCormick (*Cut*)

Chuck Palahniuk (*Fight Club*)

Jodi Picoult (*My Sister's Keeper*)

Anita Shreve

Amy Tan

Romance

Sandra Brown

Sarah Dessen (*Someone like You*)

Nicholas Sparks (*The Notebook*)

Danielle Steel

CONCLUSION

Connecting incarcerated readers with books they can enjoy is a most rewarding experience. We frequently hear "this is the first book I have ever read cover to cover" at the facilities we visit, and it never gets old. Every positive readers' advisory interaction helps encourage residents to become lifelong readers.

RESOURCES

Clark, S., and E. MacCreaigh. *Library Services to the Incarcerated: Applying the Public Library Model in Correctional Facility Libraries.* Westport, CT: Libraries Unlimited, 2006.

Clark, S., and B. Patrick. "Choose Freedom Read: Book Talks Behind Bars." *American Libraries* 30 (April 1999): 63–64.

Rubin, R. J., and D. S. Suvak. *Libraries Inside: A Practical Guide for Prison Librarians.* Jefferson, NC: McFarland, 1995.

Shirley, Glennor. "Outreach and Prisons: Connecting Inmates and Public Library Services." In *From Outreach to Equity,* edited by Robin Osborne, 20–22. Chicago: American Library Association, 2004.

21

SUGGESTING ADULT BOOKS TO TEEN READERS

Jessica E. Moyer

This chapter is for all the YA librarians working with teens who are also reading adult books, and all the adult librarians who work with teen readers at the adult services desk. In other words, this chapter is for all librarians, because all of us should be working with teen readers who enjoy and want to read adult books.

Reading adult books is common among teen readers, particularly among teens who enjoy genre fiction. Talk to any genre readers about when they started reading in their favorite genre and it was usually during the teen years.

WHY DO TEENS ENJOY ADULT GENRE FICTION?

Adult genre fiction is very attractive to teen readers: the predictable plots and stock characters that distinguish genre fiction appeal to teens, particularly those looking for predictability that is lacking in their lives, schoolbooks, or even many YA titles. Closed endings are not only common but also practically required in genre fiction. This element is uncommon in both YA literature and the literary fiction that makes up many school reading lists. Above all, teens enjoy relaxing and enjoyable reading selections just as much as adults do.

Adult genre books tend to have a reading level between seventh and ninth grade, which can make them the perfect match for many teen readers, because leisure reading is generally done two or three grade levels below ability. Avid readers often migrate to adult genre fiction looking for enough titles and lengthy enough books to keep them busy. YA titles tend to be under three hundred pages and rarely feature the drawn-out series of adult fiction, from Robert Jordan's ten-thousand-plus pages of The Wheel of Time to Anne McCaffrey's dozen-plus Pern titles or even many mystery series with ten or more titles.

Finally, science fiction and fantasy have a traditionally limited market of "YA"-specific titles. Nearly all titles are published as adult titles, with the expectation that they will be read by teens as well as adults. Although this practice has changed in recent years with the increasing growth of YA science fiction and fantasy, there are still plenty of adult titles that in another genre might be published in YA, such as John Scalzi's recent *Zoe's Tale*, which is told entirely from the point of view of a teenage girl.

Above all, there is no reason to limit teens to reading YA materials. If our job as readers' advisors is to make the match between book and reader, and the best book for the reader is not in "her" collection, that never means that it cannot be suggested. Just as many adult readers enjoy YA books (see chapter 22 in this book), so teens enjoy reading adult books.

WHY SHOULD WE HELP TEENS FIND ADULT BOOKS?

Teen readers need help in navigating adult fiction. They know little or nothing about the genre conventions, and, because it is all new to them, they may not even understand the differences between genres that are readily known to adult readers. The world of adult fiction is vast, much larger than that of either children's or YA fiction, and teens are often unsure where to start. They need guidance on titles and authors that would be best matches for them, such as books that are best for readers new to a genre, books with themes that will appeal to teen readers, and books with materials and content that are a good fit for the individual reader. Advisory for a teen reader can make (or break) a lifelong reader and genre lover, and though it can be highly rewarding, it is not the same as working with adult readers.

The first time teen readers are introduced to the adult section, they may be overwhelmed. It is the job of the readers' advisor not to compound that overwhelming feeling by pushing too many specific titles and authors at once. Passive readers' advisory techniques such as lists, displays, and bookmarks (see chapters 10 and 11) can be especially helpful, as they can be perused by the teen at her or his leisure or while browsing the collection or both. So can the RA techniques suggested by Heather Booth and Jessica Moyer:[1] placing suggested titles on a nearby shelf or table, instead of in the hands of the reader; listening carefully to a teen's interests (reading and other hobbies); suggesting and never recommending; and being specific when discussing a title, emphasizing what the book is about and why you think the reader would enjoy it.

WHEN IS IT APPROPRIATE TO SUGGEST ADULT TITLES?

If a teen reader comes to the adult services desk, there is a good chance that he or she is interested in reading adult fiction. If in talking about previous books enjoyed, the teen reader mentions adult titles, then he or she is interested in reading adult fiction. If a teen mentions having read all the books he or she liked in the YA area, then this reader is out of reading materials there and is on the hunt for adult fiction. If at any point in the conversation the teen mentions looking for books that are longer, are more complex, are part of a series, are not like school reading, or all of these, there is a good chance this reader might like adult genre fiction.

BUT WHAT ABOUT SEX, LANGUAGE, AND VIOLENCE?

Just like adults, teen readers read and enjoy books with sex, language, and violence. And just like adult readers, some teen readers prefer sweeter and tamer books. If a teen is already reading Stephen King or Laurell K. Hamilton, it is your job as advisor to find more books like that, not books that you think are more appropriate. Because teens are already used to making decisions on what they want to watch or hear or read, this is not a difficult topic to bring up in an RA interview. If you are not comfortable broaching it directly, then try these indirect approaches:

> Listen carefully to the teen's descriptions of what she has been recently watching and reading and try to match it. This approach may require knowledge of books and media outside the usual RA sphere, so a little research might be needed.

> When suggesting titles, matter-of-factly note any above-average levels of language, sex, or violence, and then let the teen choose the books he prefers.

> If you are really wary of suggesting a title but think it might be the perfect match, it is okay to ask, "Do you think your parents would have a problem with your reading this? I don't want to give you anything that might cause problems at home." In

the public and academic library, librarians are not acting in loco parentis, meaning that we are not responsible for the titles that any readers check out of our library. Make sure you're suggesting, not censoring.

WHEN IS AN ADULT BOOK A GOOD SUGGESTION FOR A TEEN READER?

Many, but not all, adult books can be good suggestions for teens, but books with at least these two qualities—younger characters and a coming-of-age theme—make for the best suggestions. Media tie-ins are also great possibilities.

Younger Characters

Books with teenage or young adult characters have perennial appeal. Such characters are one reason for the long-term popularity of adult fantasy fiction, which often features characters in their teens or early twenties. Just as children enjoy reading about characters two to three years older than they are, teenagers enjoy reading books that feature young adult characters. Science fiction also has many lead or secondary young adult characters. Romance is another genre with lots of lead characters in their teens or twenties, particularly historical and Regency romances. Other genres, such as mystery fiction, have fewer younger characters because police detectives or amateur detectives tend to be mature adults. However, sometimes these books do feature younger characters like the 11-year-old protagonist in *The Sweetness at the Bottom of the Pie* by Alan Bradley, or Mary, who is 15 at the beginning of Laurie King's Mary Russell series, which follows the young sleuth throughout her teens and twenties.

Coming-of-Age Theme

Stories that have a coming-of-age theme are also great suggestions for teen readers. Often these stories have younger characters who are becoming aware of the world around them as they search for a sense of identity. These stories are the best matches for teen readers, but books with coming-of-age themes and older characters can also work well for some teen readers.

Media Tie-Ins

One type of adult book that makes a good suggestion for teen readers is the media tie-in: a book based on a movie, TV show, or video game. Tie-ins are especially common in science fiction and fantasy: *Star Wars* and *Star Trek* both have large, popular, and long-running spin-off books, as do more recent productions like *Halo, V,* and *Jumper.* Because these are both genres that are consistently popular with teen readers, it is easy to suggest many of these titles. Media tie-ins are good suggestions for teen readers because the books are easy to read and require no prior genre knowledge. The reader is entering a known environment, with a fully developed world and usually familiar characters and story arcs. This feature allows the reader to easily step in and enjoy the story. It also makes it easier for the teen to learn about and become familiar with genre conventions without the stress of learning a completely new world and character set. These kinds of connections can work even between books. For example, teens who really enjoy Christopher Paolini's Eragon series may want to try the two adult series that inspired his work, Anne McCaffrey's Pern series and Robert Jordan's Wheel of Time series, as many of the character types, concepts, and creatures will be familiar.

TIPS FOR WORKING WITH TEENS AT THE ADULT SERVICES DESK

All adult services librarians need to be prepared to work with teen readers. Remember that this is your chance to create a lifelong leisure reader and library user. Here are several tips and ideas for success when working with teens and adult books.

> Remember that teens are generally new to reading books like these; take great care to avoid library *and* genre-related jargon.

> Suggest, don't recommend; teens have enough advice in their lives already and far too much required reading.

> Take care not to condescend; teens are very sensitive to it, especially when working with an adult authority figure.

> It's okay to note that a book has a lot of sex or violence or language or to ask during the RA interview if the teen has any preferences in these areas. Reading and looking for age-appropriate materials are not new to teen readers. At the same time, avoid suggesting only the sweetest romance or the gentlest historical

fiction. Teens enjoy books with sex and violence just as much as adults do, otherwise Stephen King wouldn't be nearly as popular as he is. For ways to approach this topic, see the "But What about Sex, Language, and Violence?" section earlier in this chapter.

Make sure teens know they can come back later for more help. Like many adults, they may not realize that readers' advisory is an important part of library services and won't want to "bother" the librarians.

Don't hesitate to approach lost-looking teens browsing the collections; offer assistance, let teens know they can ask for help, and point out bookmarks, handouts, and displays, but don't hang around and push your favorite titles.

No matter how great a book you think it is, never recommend a book to a teen with the words "I loved this when I was your age." Stick with newer books (there are plenty to choose from), and if you are lost for ideas, use the resources listed at the end of this chapter (and don't forget to share them with your patron).

TIPS FOR WORKING WITH ADULT BOOKS AT THE TEEN SERVICES DESK

Teen services librarians also need to be prepared to work with the adult book collections. In readers' advisory the goal is to match the book and the reader, even if that means working outside your usual collection. Here are several tips and ideas for working with teen readers and the adult book collection.

Know your materials. Teen services librarians should not limit themselves to reading and suggesting only YA books. They need to be familiar with at least the basics of all popular genres and with resources for finding good suggestions. Use chapter 1 of this book, "How to Read a Book in Ten Minutes," to familiarize yourself with adult genres and authors.

It is okay to refer a teen reader to the adult desk, but only if you do so carefully.

- Walk the teen over to the adult area and introduce him or her to the adult services librarians.

- Explain what the reader is looking for and why you're passing the teen off to another librarian, so everyone is on the same page.
- Make sure the teen knows that it is always okay to ask the adult services librarians for help in finding books and that he or she is still welcome to browse in the YA area and to read YA books.

When helping teens find adult titles, don't hesitate to use the RA tools designed for adult readers. Nearly all of these have YA or teen suggestions or notations or both. See the resource list at the end of this chapter for complete details.

Any professional materials on working with readers new to a genre can be adapted for teen readers.

As always, when working with teens, don't be fake. Admit it if you don't read much genre fiction or, on the other hand, if your idea of a relaxing weekend is a stack of Harlequin romances or space opera science fiction. Either way, you'll have gained your patron's trust.

Most of all, as you work with teens who enjoy reading adult books, have fun!

RESOURCES

Alex Awards are given annually by the Young Adult Library Services Association, a division of the American Library Association: www .ala.org/ala/mgrps/divs/yalsa/booklistsawards/alexawards/ alexawards.cfm. Ten adult titles, fiction and nonfiction, that especially appeal to YA readers are selected, and mainstream and literary fiction are just as likely to appear as genre fiction. A good place to start, but with only ten titles per year, good matches might not be found for all readers.

Booklist, the American Library Association's review journal, includes YA notes for all adult titles that reviewers or editors identify as having teen appeal. Several hundred titles per year are suggested here for teen readers. The advanced search feature in Booklist Online allows searching for YA notes as well as limiting by year or genre or both.

Genreflecting, nearly all the other titles in the Genreflecting series, and most adult RA tools in general make note of adult titles especially recommended for teens. These are great resources for personal browsing as well as for librarians working outside their genre knowledge or those working with teens interested in a specific genre or even subgenre. YA suggested titles can also be found in the Reader's Advisor Online database, which is based on the Genreflecting series.

School Library Journal has a section in every issue titled "Adult Books for Teens." Although it is *SLJ*'s smallest review section, the coverage is pretty good and the recommendations are excellent. A great resource for teen services librarians already using *SLJ* for YA materials.

NOTE

1. Heather Booth, *Serving Teens through Readers' Advisory* (Chicago: American Library Association, 2007); Jessica E. Moyer, "Research-Based Readers' Advisory for Teens," http://researchbasedra.pbworks.com/Research-Based-Readers% 27-Advisory-for-Teens.

22

SUGGESTING TEEN BOOKS TO ADULT READERS

Heather Booth

As the body of literature written for a teen audience has grown, so has its readership. Readers' advisors are now seeing more adults interested in reading teen fiction, and fortunately, there are many excellent options for the adult reader of teen books. In a sense, adults have always read "teen" books: the bildungsroman or coming-of-age novel is a classic genre. Adolescence is a volatile life stage that presents many rich opportunities for compelling and entertaining stories. Now that the field of YA literature is so diverse, many adults are happily feeding their interest in coming-of-age stories with books that have the appealing features of teen literature. This chapter will address why, when, and how to suggest books from your teen collection to adults, how this type of readers' advisory differs from recommending YA books to teens or adult books to adults, and the unique challenges that may arise when doing this crossover RA.

WHAT MAKES YA LIT APPEALING?

As the growing number of YA librarians might suggest, there are many adults who enjoy the literature and culture of teens. YA literature is enjoying a golden age with extraordinarily high-quality, diverse works being produced by a number of talented authors. The variety of books written for teens includes most all of the same genres written for a general audience: romance, suspense, horror, chick lit, and literary fiction. However, these books are not just mystery novels with a teen protagonist. YA literature has some distinct differences and attributes that may account for its appeal to your adult reader.

Perspective

The most defining feature of YA literature is not a teenage character; rather, it is the teenage perspective. Plenty of books are written about teens, but YA literature presents the emotions and circumstances of teens with an immediacy and empathy often absent in other coming-of-age novels. Colson Whitehead's *Sag Harbor* recalls, in rich detail, the summer its protagonist was a young teen, working his first job, negotiating new roles among friends, and experiencing the thrill of a crush. It is a vibrant recollection of youth. But the nostalgia surrounding the narrative and the past tense in which it is told separate the narrator, and thus the reader, from experiencing the events as they are happening. Instead of reacting in real time, the narrator is reflecting, impacted alternately by the wisdom, jadedness, or wistfulness that comes with age. Young adult fiction owns the feelings of teens completely. Those two-week-long relationships at 14 that we can barely recall twenty years out are depicted with sensitivity and care, as if they would last forever.

Relatively Brief Length

Though the convention is changing, teen books have traditionally been shorter than those for the general market. It is relatively easy to find a romance, historical, or suspense novel fewer than three hundred pages in the YA area that is just as entertaining as a comparable book in the adult section. Additionally, even when the page count is higher, the word count may not be.[1] YA books employ ample white space and often have smaller trim sizes, which make the reading experience seem to flow more easily.

Quick Pacing

Though Nancy Pearl's Rule of Fifty may be great for adult fiction, if a YA novel hasn't gotten off the ground and grabbed the reader in the first twenty or thirty pages, it is likely a goner. YA authors write for a discriminating audience. Unless they have to read the book for a class, teens are unlikely to give the author the same amount of time to get the story moving that an adult would. This youthful impatience means that YA books often have great hooks and first chapters that keep you reading.

Alluring Narrative Devices

As mentioned, the immediacy of the experience is a hallmark of YA literature. One way to bring this feeling to the text is to use a first-person narration. Much of YA literature has a first-person narrator. Additionally, dialogue is frequently used. This device can help make a third-person or past-tense narration more vibrant. Alternating perspectives from chapter to chapter among two or more characters is another popular technique that gives the reader the feeling of really being in the thick of the action. The slang popular in much teen fiction can also bring energy to the text.

Compressed Time Frame

Because of the relatively rapid changes a teen goes through, teen fiction tends not to span decades or years like many adult novels might. Instead, it is much more likely for a teen novel to span a school year, a summer, or an even briefer period such as a sports season or holiday break. The compressed time frame means a lot of action or character development, or both, is going to be condensed into a shorter period.

Personal Growth

To the occasional chagrin of many teens, many characters in YA literature will undergo some kind of significant personal growth or come to greater understanding about themselves or others in a way that is less common in adult fiction. Although some may classify this feature as moralizing, these frequent revelations are a common factor in teen lives. YA fiction on the lighter side (such as teen chick lit in the Gossip Girl vein) may have less of this element.

The "Cool" Factor

YA literature is hot right now. Traditionally adult authors from James Patterson to Isabel Allende have published YA novels to great success, and they are bringing their audience with them. Crossover hits like *Twilight* and *Nick and Norah's Infinite Playlist*, helped by the big-screen treatment, are introducing adults to the genre in larger numbers. Adults are realizing what so many teens already know: it's cool and fun to read YA lit!

WHEN DO WE RECOMMEND YA BOOKS TO ADULTS?

YA literature is not necessarily the first type of material that a readers' advisor might think to suggest to an adult. There are three main situations in which we will be suggesting YA materials to adults.

An adult is screening material for a child.

Many parents, teachers, and other invested adults are interested in reading the material before buying it as a gift, checking it out from the library, or adding it to a summer reading list. This situation can be very rewarding, or it can be quite challenging depending on the motivations of the adult. If the adult is open to having the child read a wide variety of material, we have an opportunity to suggest great teen books to an interested adult. This is sometimes easier than talking with a teen, as we have fewer social hurdles when talking with another adult than we might with a teen. In this situation, try to determine the motive for the adult's seeking out the material. Is the child too busy to come in? Does the parent enjoy discussing the material with the child? Or is the adult just trying to get a handle on the world of literature that the child is being exposed to?

The patron is an avid reader of YA lit.

As mentioned, YA lit is becoming a popular genre with adults. Many of them will come in looking for suggestions of other teen books to read after being captivated by one of the "blockbuster" hits. These readers tend to be lots of fun to work with, as they are excited about their discovery of a whole new section of books to read and more likely than not will be quite accepting of most suggestions. Some avid YA lit enthusiasts began reading this material as parents or teachers (see the preceding section) and got hooked. These readers tend to be more self-sufficient. If you notice them browsing with regularity, however, it might be a good opportunity to introduce them to newer authors with whom they may not yet be familiar.

It's also useful to bear in mind that some of your young*er* adult patrons (not to be confused with the *young* adults) are reading YA lit because they read it as teens and continue to enjoy it. Those in college or in their twenties often read YA lit because its familiarity appeals to them. They may be following series that began when they were younger. Or, they may have avoided YA lit as teens, but now find the stories reminding them of a "simpler" phase of their lives appealing.

A YA book fits the description of what the patron wants to read.

There are times that a patron's reading interest leads the librarian directly to a specific young adult book or to young adult literature in general. Perhaps a specific plot point may call up a historical fiction book in the teen area, or the reader desires a fantasy novel with young protagonists that is fast paced and shorter than a traditional adult fantasy novel. Readers who enjoy the attributes listed in the "What Makes YA Lit Appealing?" section of this chapter and are unfamiliar with YA literature may very well enjoy these books, but might need an introduction and a bit of coaxing to begin their exploration into this vibrant genre.

HOW DOES RECOMMENDING TEEN BOOKS TO ADULTS DIFFER FROM RECOMMENDING ADULT BOOKS TO ADULTS?

There are several key differences between suggesting teen books to adult readers and suggesting adult books to adult readers or teen books to teen readers. To obtain the best possible match, the readers' advisory transaction must include and acknowledge the following issues.

Potential bias and awkwardness must be overcome.

Some adults may be hesitant to ask for a suggestion from the teen area. Others may be hesitant to take one. Either way, acknowledging this difficulty needs to be a part of suggesting YA books to adults. Keep in mind Betty Rosenberg's First Law of Reading and pass it on to your patrons: "Never apologize for your reading tastes." We enjoy reading what we enjoy reading, regardless of what the spine label says. If the patron brings up the idea of looking in the teen section, try to make the transition in the RA interview as smooth as you would if the patron asked for suggestions set in Spain instead of France. If you as the librarian broach the subject, try presenting the book itself first, not the whole of YA literature. In the case of a patron reacting negatively to the suggestion, it might be useful to indicate *why* you selected the YA book or to mention the excellent and innovative materials being classified as YA literature these days—a far cry from what the adult may remember reading as a teen.

Other situations in which you might suggest teen material to an adult are more sensitive. Literacy or ENL (English as a new language) instructors sometimes ask about teen material for their adult students because of the assumed ease of reading. Although there are some excellent options for these adult learners in the teen area, it is important to find material that appeals to the adult's interest as well as meeting the objective of the teacher. Additionally, just because the book is in the teen area doesn't mean it will be an easy read. The ample white space and shorter length of many teen books can, at first blush, make the book appear to be a simpler read than an adult novel. But the complexity of the narrative and language can range widely.

General conventions of YA books might be unfamiliar, requiring more description or explanation.

The deceased parent, the new kid in school, the friendship that changes, the ragtag sports team—these motifs populate a good portion of teen fiction (sometimes all at once!). Someone well versed in YA literature will not bat an eye at having several books described that include such used or overused plot devices, but an adult reader not used to this convention may wonder at the repetition. Consider whether these elements really bear mentioning in the RA interaction. Having a dead, disinterested, or otherwise missing parent is prominent in YA literature partly in order to give the teen the freedom to move and act independently, without too much parental interference. Beyond this purpose, it is not necessarily a plot element that advances the story. This is not to advocate hiding the "teen-ness" of the teen fiction; rather, keep your reader in mind and select the book's appeal elements that are most applicable to your reader's interests. A savvy patron may pick up on these motifs and ask about them. In this situation, by all means encourage the conversation about the differences that he or she sees between YA and adult materials. It may lead to a discussion of appeal factors that can directly aid your suggestions.

The characters will be in a different age group.

When it comes to realistic fiction, many of us tend to suggest books with characters that we feel are similar to our patrons. We assume that the twenty-something reading the Shopaholic books or the retiree reading Agatha Raisin will need less explanation about the life of the main character because they are in a similar phase of life. Although many people do enjoy reading about characters whose lives they can relate to, we need not be bound by pairing readers with demographically similar characters.

Still, some may initially balk at the suggestion of reading about a teenage character. Remember to describe the appeal factors correctly—there has to be a good reason for suggesting the book you have chosen. If the adult is completely disinterested or turned off by the idea of reading about a teenage protagonist, the book may not be the right match.

HOW DOES RECOMMENDING TEEN BOOKS TO ADULTS DIFFER FROM RECOMMENDING TEEN BOOKS TO TEENS?

There are several key differences between recommending a YA book to a teen reader and suggesting the same book to an adult reader. Here are three things to keep in mind when suggesting YA titles to adult readers.

It is likely *not* a homework assignment.

When we do readers' advisory with teenagers, we are constantly walking a line between meeting their needs as students and meeting their interests as readers. Perhaps the perfect book for a teen reader might be twenty pages shy of a length requirement, or it hits the mark for appeal and length but is set in the wrong historical period. When suggesting YA books to adults, we are largely freed from these requirements. This enables us to focus solely on interest and appeal.

Sex and foul language may not be as much of a consideration, but then again . . .

Just as our suggestions to adults are not bound by assignment requirements, we may not need to be as cautious as we otherwise might regarding sex and sexuality, coarse language, and other potentially objectionable content. Adults are more likely to be up front when asked if they are bothered by "spicier" reads or if they prefer a gentler story. When the readers' advisor and patron are able to speak as peers, it is easier to suss out the nuance of the patron's tolerance of such content.

It is important to remember, though, that today's realistic teen stories, especially those in the "problem novel" genre, and those teen chick lit series describing the bad behavior of the social elite can be just as shocking and gritty as anything in the general fiction section. Adults hoping for a kinder, gentler romance may not necessarily find what they are looking for if they stumble upon today's teen fiction. Also, although teen fans of problem novels are largely open to reading about young people in dangerous or negative situations, with bleak outlooks and a lack of positive role models, some adult readers may feel that this heavier material is best left unread.

Adults may be less familiar with the authors and subgenres.

Even though YA literature is growing in popularity among a wide range of readers, most of its adult readership does not have the benefit that teens do of seeing their friends' free reading selections every day in school. Adults will likely be less familiar with popular authors, beyond the superstars like J. K. Rowling and Stephenie Meyer. They may also be surprised to find that there were many teen supernatural romances before *Twilight* hit it big and that there have been many since, or that a great number of authors popular with teens write novels exclusively in free verse. The contemporary "classics" that many teens have been exposed to through school such as Laurie Halse Anderson's *Speak* or Louis Sachar's *Holes* are touch points that we can use to connect teens to other similar or dissimilar books. Adults new to reading YA material will likely not have experienced these books. If they are interested in reading what the teens are reading, by all means expose them to the required or suggested reading lists for your local school districts!

THE TERMINOLOGY OF YA VERSUS ADULT LITERATURE

Some terms commonly used in both adult and teen works may need some clarification when doing crossover advisory.

> *Angst/angsty.* Teen angst! There's nothing like it for bringing a dose of realism to YA novels. But adult readers who are unfamiliar with the highly emotional, sometimes whiny characters who people teen literature may have a lower tolerance for angst. A character that we might describe to a teen as goofy and kind of offbeat may come across as a complainer to an adult who is used to reading about composed, emotionally mature characters.
>
> *Coming-of-age.* As mentioned previously, novels in which young people come of age are not the sole domain of YA literature. Adult readers looking for a coming-of-age story and desiring

to read YA literature will likely have many more options if they don't limit their search just to books that are described as "coming-of-age" novels. Most characters in YA lit undergo some type of loss of innocence or burgeoning self-awareness common in coming-of-age.

Mystery. Adult mysteries follow fairly clear-cut conventions: a crime or body is uncovered, a detective investigates, the crime is solved. When a YA novel is deemed a *mystery,* it may be similar to the classic definition, but the term may also describe a suspense novel, one with a paranormal element, or just a "mysterious" feeling.

Young adult. This term is subject to dispute from time to time: how young does it start and how old does it go? It seems like the borders are ever broadening, but the term generally encompasses those ages 12 through 18, sometimes creeping down to 10 or 11 and up through the college years.

TOOLS AND RESOURCES

The following are excellent sources to which you can turn when looking for young adult books that will appeal to your adult readers.

Best Books for Young Adults (YALSA). www.ala.org/yalsa/ booklists/bbya. These annual lists select books for "proven or potential appeal to the personal reading tastes of the young adult." They are books that either have already become popular with teens or contain the qualities that could likely make them popular. For those adult readers who enjoy YA literature, this is a good place to look for current fiction and nonfiction.

Booklist Online. www.booklistonline.com. A subscription database with the full text of all *Booklist* reviews since 1990. Use the advanced search to locate YA titles with adult appeal in thousands of *Booklist* reviews.

Hahn, Daniel, et al., eds. *The Ultimate Teen Book Guide.* New York: Walker, 2007. Unlike many readers' advisory resource books, this volume suggests adult and young adult books indiscriminately. Each book listed is accompanied by suggestions for several additional titles that might appeal. This is a good place to start with a reader who can recall a book he or she enjoyed. Begin by looking that book up and seeing what YA books are listed as suggested reads.

NoveList or Reader's Advisor Online. These subscription databases are useful places to search for teen material with adult appeal based on plot points, especially if you are not familiar with much of the teen collection. Searching for terms describing the plot and limiting the search to teen materials will yield titles that you and your patron can explore as potential matches.

Squicciarini, Stephanie A., and Susan Person. "Young Adult Literature: Not Just for Teens Anymore." *VOYA* (June 2008): 106–109. http://pdfs.voya.com/VO/YA2/VOYA200806YALit.pdf. A useful list of over fifty YA books with potential adult appeal across a variety of genres. Most were published within the last ten years, and starred authors have written multiple titles that adults will likely be interested in.

Vibrant communities of readers are coming together online through sites like Goodreads (www.goodreads.com) or LibraryThing (www.librarything.com), where searching "YA books for adults" yields titles that *actual* adults who enjoy YA literature have read and enjoyed enough to tag as such. These from-the-horse's-mouth recommendations vary widely, but they can show your adult reader the diversity of YA books enjoyed by her or his contemporaries.

Note

1. Don Gallo, "Help! Books Are Growing on Us!" *Voice of Youth Advocates* 32 (June 2009): 118–121.

CONTRIBUTORS

Alicia Ahlvers is branch manager for the Waldo Community Branch of the Kansas City Public Library. She is also chair of the Notable Books Council for 2009–2010.

Sue-Ellen Beauregard is media editor of *Booklist,* a publication of the American Library Association and sponsor of the ALA Odyssey Award for Excellence in Audiobook Production. In addition to her editing duties, Beauregard serves as consultant to the Odyssey Award and to several ALA Notable media committees. She is a judge for the Audie Awards and for the past two years has served on the panel to choose the Best Audiobook of the Year. She received her master of arts degree in library science from the University of Wisconsin–Milwaukee.

Heather Booth is the teen services librarian at the Thomas Ford Memorial Library in Western Springs, Illinois. Her book, *Serving Teens through Readers' Advisory* (American Library Association, 2007), was a *VOYA* Five-Foot Bookshelf pick. She reviews books for youth and audiobooks for *Booklist* magazine and frequently writes about teen services and readers' advisory issues.

Sarah Statz Cords has worked as an academic librarian for the University of Wisconsin–Madison and as a public library assistant in the Madison (Wisconsin) Public Library. She has taught courses on the reading interests of adults for the UW–Madison School of Library and Information Studies and is the author of *The Public Speaking Handbook for Librarians and Information Professionals, The Real Story: A Guide to Nonfiction Reading Interests, The Inside Scoop: A Guide to Nonfiction Investigative Writing and Exposés,* and *Now Read This III* (with Nancy Pearl). She is an associate editor for the Reader's Advisor Online database and writes for its blog at www.readersadvisoronline.com. Her nonfiction review blog can be found at www.citizenreader.com.

Erin Downey Howerton holds an MA in English from Kansas State University and an MLIS from Florida State University. She is currently the school liaison at Johnson County Library in Overland Park, Kansas. Howerton has worked with youth for nearly a decade in both library

and higher education settings. She has published various articles and
book chapters about library collections, intellectual freedom, and
technology topics. Howerton blogs about education, libraries, and
technology at http://schoolingdotus.blogspot.com and maintains an
educational wiki at http://cyber64edu.wetpaint.com.

Lucy M. Lockley is collection development manager for St. Charles
(Missouri) City-County Library District. She coordinates the district's
readers' advisory team and developed the Multi-Genre Book Discussion Program for training staff in readers' advisory tools and
techniques. She has presented nationally on genre study, readers'
advisory, and fund-raising through trivia night events. She wrote a
collection development article on disabilities for *Library Journal* in
1999 and in 2009 was a presenter for a *Library Journal*/Thorndike Press
webcast on best practices in large print collection development.

Bobbi Newman is dedicated to helping libraries find their place in the
digital age and has traveled far and wide to share and exchange
information. She has trained patrons and library staff about using
new and emerging technologies in their lives. She is a librarian,
teacher, presenter, writer, photographer, and video game junkie. She
also writes at http://librarianbyday.net.

Kate Pickett is the young adult librarian for the Johnson County Library
in Overland Park, Kansas. She participates in several programs for
incarcerated teens, including Read to Succeed, a short-story discussion
group at the Juvenile Detention Center where residents can talk about
what they are reading and select from donated books, and Changing
Lives through Literature, a book group for juvenile offenders in which
participants discuss six books over the course of seven weeks with a
facilitator, a parole officer, and a judge.

Paul Smith is a communications specialist in the Public Affairs Department of the Kansas City (Missouri) Public Library, which earned a
National Medal from IMLS in 2008 due in large part to the quality
of its public events. A former journalist, Smith earned a Robert F.
Kennedy Journalism Award in 2002.

Kay Sodowsky is a proud graduate of the University of Kansas and the
University of Illinois Graduate School of Library and Information
Science. She has worked in public, university, and community
college libraries and was the associate editor of *Olderr's Fiction Index.*
Sodowsky loves working with book groups and enjoys coordinating

diversity programming for the community college. She lives in suburban Kansas City, Missouri.

Lissa Staley has worked as a public services librarian and book evangelist at the Topeka and Shawnee County (Kansas) Public Library since 2001. Locally renowned as the host of the library's Trivia Night, she blogs at www.tscpl.org. Staley's ideal book would include jacket copy comparing it to Douglas Adams, Kurt Vonnegut, or Connie Willis.

CJ Sullivan is the outreach coordinator for the Johnson County Library in Overland Park, Kansas. She is responsible for day-to-day coordination and operation of library outreach services and personally facilitates short-story and book discussion groups with residents in correctional facilities. She works with the Friends of the Library to select donated and weeded materials for resident bookshelves and libraries in jails and residential centers.

Lynne Welch is the reference librarian at Herrick Memorial Library of Wellington, Ohio, and was named the 2004 Librarian of the Year by the Romance Writers of America. She reviews popular fiction for *Booklist* and contributes read-alikes and themed booklists to the EBSCOhost/ NoveList and NoveList Plus readers' advisory databases.

David Wright works as a fiction librarian at Seattle Public Library's Central branch and helps edit the library's blog, *Shelf Talk*. He has written columns, articles, and book reviews for a variety of library media, including *Booklist* ("He Reads"), NoveList ("Hot Topics"), *RUSQ*, and *Library Journal*, and he contributed the chapter "Zen and the Art of Readers' Advisory" to ALA's *Research-Based Readers' Advisory*. He has served on ALA's and PLA's readers' advisory committees and has spoken at library and literary conferences from Toronto to Anchorage, New York to Los Angeles. In previous lives, Wright has been a goatherd, a harlot, a stereopticon salesman, and, oddly enough, a librarian.

Jessica Zellers, who is descended from a line of zombies, is the electronic resources librarian at the Williamsburg Regional Library in Virginia. She helped found the library's award-winning book review blog, *Blogging for a Good Book* (http://bfgb.wordpress.com), and writes Author Read-Alikes for NoveList. She enjoys writing for her own website at thelesbrarian.com and reads a lot of graphic novels, ostensibly for professional development.

INDEX